Penguin
LIVES

Marcel Proust

A LIPPER/VIKING BOOK

EDMUND WHITE

Marcel Proust

A Penguin Life

A LIPPER/VIKING BOOK

VIKING

Published by the Penguin Group

Penguin Putnam Inc., 375 Hudson Street, New York, New York 10014, U.S.A.
Penguin Books Ltd, 27 Wrights Lane, London W8 5TZ, England
Penguin Books Australia Ltd, Ringwood, Victoria, Australia
Penguin Books Canada Ltd, 10 Alcorn Avenue, Toronto, Ontario, Canada M4V 3B2
Penguin Books (N.Z.) Ltd, 182–190 Wairau Road, Auckland 10, New Zealand
Penguin India, 210 Chiranjiv Tower, 43 Nehru Place, New Delhi, 11009, India

Penguin Books Ltd, Registered Offices:
Harmondsworth, Middlesex, England

First published in 1999 by Viking Penguin,
a member of Penguin Putnam Inc.

5   7   9   10   8   6   4

Acknowledgment is made to *Marcel Proust* by Jean-Yves Tadié
(Gallimard, 1996) as a valuable resource in the preparation of this work.

LIBRARY OF CONGRESS CATALOGING-IN-PUBLICATION DATA
White, Edmund.
Marcel Proust / Edmund White.
p.   cm.
"A Penguin life."
Includes bibliographical references.
ISBN 0-670-88057-4
1. Proust, Marcel, 1871–1922.   2. Novelists, French—20th century—
Biography.   I. Title.
PQ2631.R63Z982   1999
843'.912—dc21   98-22119
[B]

This book is printed on acid-free paper.

Printed in the United States of America
Set in Fournier
Designed by Francesca Belanger

to Marie-Claude de Brunhoff

Marcel Proust

I

IN ENGLAND not long ago a survey of writers and critics revealed that the twentieth-century novelist they most admired—and who they thought would have the most enduring influence on the next century—was Marcel Proust. Certainly the madeleine moistened by herbal tea has become the most famous symbol in French literature; everyone refers to sudden gusts of memory as "Proustian experiences." Snobs like to point out that if the Prousts had been better-mannered and not given to dunking, world literature would have been the poorer for it. Even those who haven't read Proust speak of him freely and often.

Studying him, of course, can have a disastrous effect on a young writer, who either comes under the influence of Proust's dangerously idiosyncratic and contagious style or who feels that Proust has already done everything possible in the novel form. Even Walter Benjamin, who became Proust's German translator, wrote the philosopher Theodor Adorno that he did not want to read one more word by Proust than was actually necessary for him to translate because otherwise he would become addictively dependent, which would be an obstacle to his own production.

Graham Greene once wrote: "Proust was the greatest novelist of the twentieth century, just as Tolstoy was in the nineteenth. . . . For those who began to write at the end of the twenties or the beginning of the thirties, there were two great inescapable influences: Proust and Freud, who are mutually complementary." Certainly Proust's fame and prestige have eclipsed those of Joyce, Beckett, Virginia Woolf and Faulkner, of Hemingway and Fitzgerald, of Gide and Valéry and Genet, of Thomas Mann and Bertolt Brecht, for if some of these writers are more celebrated than Proust in their own country, Proust is the only one to have a uniformly international reputation. The young Andrew Holleran, who would go on to publish the most important American gay novel of the seventies, *Dancer from the Dance*, wrote a friend eight years earlier: "Robert, much has happened: That is, I finally finished *Remembrance of Things Past* and I don't know what to say—the idea that Joyce ended the novel is so absurd; it's Proust who ended the novel, simply by doing something so complete, monumental, perfect, that what the fuck can you do afterwards?"

Joyce met Proust once and they exchanged scarcely a word, even though they shared a cab together (neither had read the other). Beckett wrote a small critical book about Proust; Woolf admired Proust so intensely that she felt swamped by his genius. Gide's bitterest regret was that as a founder of a fledgling but already prestigious publishing

2

house, he turned down *Swann's Way*, the first volume of Proust's masterpiece (he thought of Proust as a superficial snob and a mere reporter of high-society events). Genet began to write his first novel, *Our Lady of the Flowers*, after reading the opening pages of Proust's *Within a Budding Grove*. Genet was in prison and he arrived late in the exercise yard for the weekly book exchange; as a result he was forced to take the one book all the other prisoners had rejected. And yet once he'd read the opening pages of Proust he shut the book, wanting to savor every paragraph over as long a period as possible. He said to himself: "Now, I'm tranquil, I know I'm going to go from marvel to marvel." His reading inspired him to write; he hoped to become the Proust of the underclass.

And yet Proust was not always so appreciated, and even his chief defenders were capable of making snide remarks about him. Robert de Montesquiou (whose arch manners and swooping intonations Proust loved to imitate and whose life provided Proust with the main model for his most memorable character, the baron de Charlus) said that Proust's work was "a mixture of litanies and sperm" (a formula that he considered to be a compliment). Gide accused him of having committed "an offense against the truth" (Gide was irritated that Proust never acknowledged his own homosexuality in print nor ever presented homosexual inclinations in an attractive light). Lucien Daudet, a young writer with whom Proust had an affair (Proust liked artistic young men with mustaches and dark eyes: that is, those who resembled himself), at one point told Cocteau that Proust was "an atrocious insect." Lucien's father, Alphonse Daudet, one of the most celebrated writers of the generation before Proust's, though now largely forgotten, announced, "Marcel Proust is the devil!" He might well have taken such a position, since it was Proust's seven-volume novel, *Remembrance of Things Past* (in recent editions, translated more literally as *In Search of Lost Time*), that surpassed—indeed, wiped out—the fiction written in the two decades before him. Who today reads Anatole France, Paul Bourget, Maurice Barrès, or even Alphonse Daudet? Paul Claudel, the arch-Catholic poet and playwright, described Marcel as "a painted old Jewess." In New York during the 1970s one popular T-shirt, using the Yiddish word for a female gossip, brandished the slogan "Proust Is a Yenta"!

These insults, many of them handed out by people who on alternate days adored Proust, were neutralized by an issue of *La Nouvelle Revue Française*, France's best literary magazine at the time, that was entirely dedicated to Proust. It came out in 1923, just a year after Proust's death, and contained photos of the dead master, previously unpublished snippets from his pen, and evaluations from critics, French but also from nations all over the world. Most touching were the many personal testimonies. The poet Anna de Noailles, herself a monument to egotism, praised Proust for his ... modesty. (The duc de Gramont, one of Proust's highest-born friends, once remarked that aristocrats invited Proust for country weekends not because of his art but because he and Anna de Noailles were the two funniest people in Paris.)

Everyone had a sharp memory to share. Jean Cocteau, the poet-playwright-impresario-filmmaker *(Beauty and the Beast)*, recalled Proust's voice: "Just as the voice of a ventriloquist comes out of his chest, so Proust's emerged from his soul." The writer Léon-Paul Fargue remembered seeing Proust towards the end of his life, "completely pale, with his hair down to his eyebrows, his beard, so black it was blue, devouring his face. . . ." Fargue noticed the long sleeves covering frozen hands, the Persian, almond-shaped eyes. "He looked like a man who no longer lives outdoors or by day, a hermit who hasn't emerged from his oak tree for a long time, with something pained about the face, the expression of suffering that has just begun to be calmed. He seemed possessed by a bitter goodness." A young aristocratic woman recalled that when she was a girl she was supposed to be presented to him at a ball, but the great writer, "livid and bearded," wearing the collar of his overcoat turned up, stared at her with such intensity that when they were finally introduced she was so frightened she nearly fainted.

One of Proust's ex-lovers and his most constant friend, Reynaldo Hahn, the composer, recalled that soon after he met Proust they were walking through a garden when suddenly Proust stopped dead before a rosebush. He asked Hahn to continue walking without him. When at last Hahn circled back, after going around the château, "I found him at the same place, staring at the roses. His head tilting forward, his face very serious, he blinked, his eyebrows slightly furrowed as though from a passionate act of attention, and with his left hand he was obstinately pushing the end of his little black mustache between his lips and nibbling on it. . . . How many times I've observed Marcel in these mysterious moments in which he was communicating totally with nature, with art, with life, in these 'deep minutes' in which his entire being was concentrated. . . ." Typically, Proust also invoked this very scene, but said that inhaling the moment was ineffectual; only the sudden, unprompted awakenings of memory, triggered by something illogical and unforeseen (the madeleine, for example), could invoke the past in its entirety.

The great Colette completely failed to sense his value when she first ran into Proust (they were both very young and just starting out as writers). She'd even gone so far, in one of her early Claudine novels, as to call him a "yid" *(youpin)*, but her husband urbanely crossed out the insult and replaced it with "boy" *(garçon)*. Even cleaned up, the passage doesn't make for very pleasant reading. It states that at a literary salon, "I was pursued, politely, all evening by a young and pretty boy of letters." Because of her cropped hair, unusual for the period, he kept comparing her to the young god Hermes or to a cupid drawn by Prud'hon. "My little flatterer, excited by his own evocations, wouldn't leave me alone for a second. . . . He gazed at me with caressing, long-lashed eyes. . . ." At the same time, in 1895, she wrote Proust a letter in which she acknowledged that he had recognized a crucial truth: "The word is not a representation but a living thing, and it is much less a mnemonic sign than a pictorial translation."

Perhaps Colette had been initially irritated because the young flatterer had already divined her bisexuality. By 1917, after Proust had begun to publish *Remembrance of Things Past*, she could see him in another light. He was very ill, he weighed no more than one hundred pounds, and he seldom emerged from his cork-lined room. He had become a martyr to art (and she herself was one of his few living rivals as a stylist). She saw him at the Ritz during the war with a few friends, wearing a fur coat even indoors over his evening clothes: "He never stopped talking, trying to be gay. Because of the cold, and making excuses, he kept his top hat on, tilted backwards, and the fan-like lock of hair covered his eyebrows. Full-dress uniform, but disarranged by a furious wind, which, pouring over the nape of his hat, rumpling the calico and the free ends of his cravat, filling in with a grey ash the furrows of his cheeks, the hollows of his eye-sockets and the breathless mouth, had hunted this tottering young man of fifty to death."

These portraits already suggest the outlines of Proust's extraordinary personality. He was attentive to his friends to the point of seeming a flatterer, though he thought friendship was valueless and conversation represented the death of the mind, since he believed only passion and suffering could sharpen the powers of observation and the only word of any value was the written. He could stare transfixed at a rose—or at anything else or anyone who was on his peculiar wavelength—but though he read everything and was deeply cultivated, he had little interest in disembodied ideas. He wasn't an intellectual, though he was supremely intelligent. He applied his attention to flowers and people and paintings, but not to theories about botany nor to psychology nor aesthetics. He never read a word of Freud, for instance (nor did Freud ever read a word of Proust). He was hilariously funny and entertaining, but he emanated a calm spirituality except, perhaps, when he was doubled up with a crazy bout of laughter (his famous choking fit of hilarity, his *fou rire,* which could go on so long it struck strangers as weird, even slightly mad). He was such a presence that many people spoke of him as tall, but in fact he stood just five feet six inches.

Marcel Proust was the son of a Christian father and a Jewish mother. He himself was baptized (on August 5, 1871, at the church of Saint-Louis d'Antin) and later confirmed as a Catholic, but he never practiced that faith and as an adult could best be described as a mystical atheist, someone imbued with spirituality who nonetheless did not believe in a personal God, much less in a savior. Although Jews trace their religion through their mothers, Proust never considered himself Jewish and even became vexed when a newspaper article listed him as a Jewish author. His father once warned him not to stay in a certain hotel since there were "too many" Jewish guests there, and, to be sure, in *Remembrance of Things Past* there are unflattering caricatures of the members of one Jewish family, the Blochs. Jews were still considered exotic, even "oriental," in France; in 1872 there were only eighty-six thousand Jews in the whole country. In a typically offensive passage Proust writes that in a French drawing room "a Jew making his entry as though he were emerging from the desert, his body crouching like a hyena's, his neck thrust forward, offering profound 'salaams,' completely satisfies a certain taste for the oriental."

Proust never refers to his Jewish origins in his fiction, although in the youthful novel he abandoned, *Jean Santeuil* (first published only in 1952, thirty years after his death), there is a very striking, if buried, reference to Judaism. The autobiographical hero has quarreled with his parents and in his rage deliberately smashed a piece of delicate Venetian glass his mother had given him. When he and his mother are reconciled, he tells her what he has done: "He expected that she would scold him, and so revive in his mind the memory of their quarrel. But there was no cloud upon her tenderness. She gave him a kiss, and whispered in his ear: 'It shall be, as in the Temple, the symbol of an indestructible union.' " This reference to the rite of smashing a glass during the Orthodox Jewish wedding ceremony, in this case sealing the marriage of mother to son, is not only spontaneous but chilling. In an essay about his mother he referred, with characteristic ambiguity, to "the beautiful lines of her Jewish face, completely marked with Christian sweetness and Jansenist resignation, turning her into Esther herself"—a reference, significantly, to the heroine of the Old Testament (and of Racine's play), who concealed her Jewish identity until she had become the wife of King Ahasuerus and was in a position to save her people. The apparently gentile Proust, who had campaigned for Dreyfus and had been baptized Catholic, was a sort of modern Esther.

Despite Proust's silences and lapses on the subject of his mother's religion, it would be unfair, especially in light of the rampant anti-Semitism of turn-of-the-century France, to say that he was unique or even extreme in his prejudice against Jews. And yet his anti-Semitism is more than curious, given his love for his mother and given, after her death, something very much like a religious cult that he developed around her. His mother, out of respect for her parents, had remained faithful to their religion, and Proust revered her and her relatives; after her death he regretted that he was too ill to visit her grave and the graves of her parents and uncle in the Jewish cemetery and to mark each visit with a stone. More important, although he had many friends among the aristocracy whom he had assiduously cultivated, nevertheless when he was forced to take sides during the Dreyfus Affair, which had begun in 1894 and erupted in 1898, he chose to sign a petition prominently printed in a newspaper calling for a retrial.

The Dreyfus Affair is worth a short detour, since it split

French society for many years and it became a major topic in Proust's life—and in *Remembrance of Things Past*. Alfred Dreyfus (1859–1935) was a Jew and a captain in the French army. In December 1894 he was condemned by a military court for having sold military secrets to the Germans and was sent for life to Devil's Island. The accusation was based on the evidence of a memorandum stolen from the German embassy in Paris (despite the fact that the writing did not resemble Dreyfus's) and of a dossier (which was kept classified and secret) handed over to the military court by the minister of war. In 1896 another French soldier, Major Georges Picquart, proved that the memorandum had been written not by Dreyfus but by a certain Major Marie Charles Esterhazy. Yet Esterhazy was acquitted and Picquart was imprisoned. Instantly a large part of the population called for a retrial of Dreyfus. On January 13, 1898, the writer Emile Zola published an open letter, "J'accuse," directed against the army's general staff; Zola was tried and found guilty of besmirching the reputation of the army. He was forced to flee to England. Then in September 1898 it was proved that the only piece of evidence against Dreyfus in the secret military dossier had been faked by Joseph Henry, who confessed his misdeed and committed suicide. At last the government ordered a retrial of Dreyfus. Public opinion was bitterly divided between the leftist Dreyfusards, who demanded "justice and truth," and the anti-Dreyfusards, who led an anti-Semitic campaign, defended the honor of the army, and rejected the call for a retrial. The conflict led to a virtual civil war. In 1899 Dreyfus was found guilty again, although this time under extenuating circumstances—and the president pardoned him. Only in 1906 was Dreyfus fully rehabilitated, named an officer once again, and decorated with the Legion of Honor. Interestingly, Theodor Herzl, the Paris correspondent for a Viennese newspaper, was so overwhelmed by the virulent anti-Semitism of the Dreyfus Affair that he was inspired by the prophetic idea of a Jewish state.

In defending Dreyfus, Proust not only angered conservative, Catholic, pro-army aristocrats, but he also alienated his own father. In writing about the 1890s in *Remembrance of Things Past*, Proust remarks that "the Dreyfus case was shortly to relegate the Jews to the lowest rung of the social ladder." Typically, the ultraconservative Gustave Schlumberger, a great Byzantine scholar, could give in his posthumous memoirs as offensive a description of his old friend Charles Haas (a model for Proust's character Swann) as this: "The delightful Charles Haas, the most likeable and glittering socialite, the best of friends, had nothing Jewish about him except his origins and was not afflicted, as far as I know, with any of the faults of his race, which makes him an exception virtually unique." It would be misleading to suggest that Proust took his controversial, pro-Dreyfus stand simply because he was half-Jewish. No, he was only obeying the dictates of his conscience, even though he lost many highborn Catholic friends by doing so and exposed himself to the snide anti-Semitic accusation of merely automatically siding with his co-religionists.

Marcel Proust was born on July 10, 1871, to well-to-do middle-class parents. His mother was Jeanne Weil, a twenty-one-year-old Parisian, daughter of Nathé Weil, a rich stockbroker. Her great-uncle Adolphe Crémieux was a senator and received a state funeral; he was also president of the Universal Israelite Alliance. Her mother, Adèle, was (like the Narrator's grandmother in *Remembrance of Things Past*) a cultured woman who loved, above all other literature, the letters of Madame de Sévigné, one of Louis XIV's courtiers and a woman who was almost romantically in love with her own daughter (the one-sided Sévigné mother-daughter relationship inspired Thornton Wilder when he wrote *The Bridge of San Luis Rey*). This intense intimacy was in fact characteristic of Marcel and his own mother, who were inseparable, who fought frequently (usually over his laziness and lack of willpower) but always fell into each other's arms as soon as they made up. Mother and son shared a love of music and literature; she could speak and read German as well as English. She had a perfect memory and knew long passages from Racine by heart; her dying words were a citation from La Fontaine: "If you're not a Roman, at least act worthy of being one." Marcel inherited her taste for memorizing poetry and knew long passages from Victor Hugo, Racine, and Baudelaire. Most important, Marcel and his mother both loved to laugh—gently, satirically—at the people around them, and in her letters to him she sends up the other guests at a spa or hotel with the same spirit of wickedly close observation and good-natured if prickly fun that was to inspire so many of his best pages.

Proust's father, Adrien, thirty-five years old when Marcel was born, came from a far more humble background, though he rose to great heights in the medical profession. His father had been a grocer in Illiers (the name is derived from that of Saint Hilaire), a village near the cathedral town of Chartres, south of Paris; Marcel gave the village the name of "Combray," and today it is known officially as Illiers-Combray and has become a major goal for Proust pilgrims from all over the world. (The local bakeries are all grinding out madeleines in Proust's honor, and the house where he and his family summered has become a museum. Perhaps in another century the name Illiers will be dropped altogether as life completely surrenders to the tyranny of art.)

Adrien Proust was originally intended for the priesthood and he brought a nearly religious zeal to his work as a doctor. It was he who made famous—and effective—the idea of a *cordon sanitaire*, a "sanitary zone" circling Europe in order to keep out cholera. In order to put his principles to work Dr. Proust traveled to Russia, Turkey, and Persia in 1869 and figured out the routes by which cholera in previous epidemics had entered Russia and thereby Europe. For this successful investigation and the resulting efficacious sanitation and quarantine campaign Dr. Proust was awarded the Legion of Honor. He became one of the most celebrated professors of medicine and practicing physicians of his day. Whereas Marcel would be willowy, artistic, asthmatic, and obsessed with titled ladies, his father was the very model of the solid upper-middle-class citizen, fleshy, bearded, solemn, and, thanks to his wife's fortune, rich. He was also, unbeknownst to his son, an inveterate ladies' man. His extramarital adventures were never noticed by Marcel's mother—or if she did know something about them, she was too discreet to mention it.

In the partially autobiographical novel *Jean Santeuil*, written while his parents were still alive, Marcel portrays his father as a brute ("What a vulgar man," thinks Jean Santeuil), someone whose peasant ways had not been amended by a lifetime of honors. In his correspondence Marcel later told his editor that his father had tried to cure him of his effeminacy and neuroses by sending him to a whorehouse. But by the time he came to write *Remembrance of Things Past*, after his parents' death, he idealized both of them and disguised his father as a wise, indulgent minister of state.

Proust's mother was pregnant with him during the Franco-Prussian War and the difficult aftermath of France's defeat, the period when Napoleon III was chased from the throne and a socialist commune was briefly declared in Paris before the Third Republic was at last established. During the months of war and the internecine street fighting, coal and wood supplies ran out and houses went unheated. In

Paris the starving populace ate dogs and cats, even the animals in the zoo. As a result, Jeanne Proust was so weakened from hunger and anxiety that when Marcel was born he was sickly and fragile and at first not expected to live.

In this respect, as in so many others, Marcel was the opposite of his hearty, healthy brother, Robert, born two years later, on May 24, 1873, in more prosperous and settled times. The two brothers were perfect companions as children and remained very close all their lives, although it was the robust younger brother, Robert, who often played the role of protector to the asthmatic Marcel. Like his father, Robert became a doctor—and a womanizer—yet the two brothers never quarreled, and lived their whole lives in the most complete harmony. In the 1890s both brothers were Dreyfusards. At the end of his life Marcel asked Robert to intervene and secure for him the Legion of Honor and, once this honor was obtained, to confer it on him. Robert was at Marcel's bedside when he died, and after his death it was Robert who oversaw the publication of the last two volumes of his masterpiece as well as his selected correspondence.

As a little boy Marcel could not go to sleep without his mother's kiss; this necessity would become a major theme of "Combray," the first section of *Remembrance of Things Past*. Quite understandably she was worried by these signs of her son's total dependence on her and would attempt to cure him by refusing to indulge him in his "whims," but he would become so hysterical if denied a kiss or his mother's tenth "good night" visit to his bedroom that usually she gave in—or her less rigorous husband would urge her to do so. Not only did Proust not outgrow his dependence; it became the template for his adult loves, since for Proust passion was a nagging need that became only more demanding the more it was denied. Indeed, Proust would drive away all his lovers (in his fiction as in his life) through his unreasonable demands.

II

PROUST GREW UP in the then recently constructed Paris built by the baron Haussmann, Napoleon III's master town planner—a spacious, bourgeois world of broad boulevards radiating out from the Arc de Triomphe and the Champs-Elysées, a web of tree-lined streets of nearly identical façades of seven-story apartment buildings constructed out of pale stone and wrought-iron balconies. Inside, the apartments were huge, with massive reception rooms, creaking parquet floors, machine-cast plaster ornaments on the ceilings, white marble fireplaces, a rabbit warren of servants' quarters, and all the modern conveniences. By the time Marcel was three his family was living at 9 boulevard Malesherbes, where they enjoyed running water, gas lighting, central heating from a coal furnace, toilets, a large bathroom, a wide, well-lit stair-case with marble steps and a wrought-iron banister, even an elevator. Dr. Proust was delighted with the airy apartment, in which the parents' room was separated from the children's quarters by a corridor some forty-five feet long. He judged it to be hygienic, modern, and comfortable—his highest praise.

Marcel himself considered their family salon to be of "an ugliness completely medical." And Marcel's school friend Fernand Gregh later wrote of the Proust apartment: "The impression I've kept, and that I see again when I close my eyes, is of a rather dark interior, bursting with heavy furniture, weatherstripped with curtains, stuffed with carpets, everything black and red, the Platonic apartment, not really that far removed from the somber bric-à-brac of Balzac's time." It was a seven-room apartment, with Dr. Proust's consulting room on one side of the living room, and on the other, Proust's bedroom, redolent of his eucalyptus fumigations, considered useful in treating the symptoms of asthma.

This was the Paris of new, giant department stores; of the recently built Palais Garnier opera house, which resembles a cross between a Victorian inkwell and a Liechtenstein medal for bravery; of newspaper kiosks and Morris columns (those turreted, freestanding, upended tubes on which theater posters are glued); of omnibuses (horse-drawn public vehicles) and *vespassiennes* (ornate public urinals, and occasional gay cruising grounds). As a boy Proust would run out every morning to see which plays were being advertised by the posters on the Morris column across the street (it's still there in front of 8 boulevard Malesherbes). This was the Paris in which aristocratic women sporting diamonds and ostrich plumes and men in top hats and tails rode through the streets at night in their elegant carriages to balls or private dinners. At receptions there was inevitably one footman for every three guests—and the footmen had to be at least five feet ten inches tall. (The upper-middle-class Prousts kept a live-in butler, chambermaid, and cook.) In the houses of the rich and aristocratic, the comfortable family side of the living quarters was rigidly separated from the formal reception rooms. Men of this class smoked cigars banded with personalized gilt paper rings and had their shirts sent to be washed and pressed in London. The rich attended the opera, where often they arrived late and left early, staying only long enough during the third act to visit their friends in their boxes, to see and be seen, and to watch the ballet (some of the dancers were kept by the fashionable male members of the exclusive Jockey Club). This was the Paris of the Bois de Boulogne, the vast park west of Paris where rich women, members of society and of the demimonde, were slowly drawn down the shaded, well-sanded, and well-watered roads in their carriages as they received the nods and salutes of men on horseback or on foot. An evening outing in the Bois was one of the few daily rituals everyone observed. This was the Paris of the Impressionists, of well-manicured gardens and children playing with stick and hoop. But it was also the Paris of the newly erected (and much criticized) Eiffel Tower, of train stations with glass and metal roofs, of great financiers speculating on the next building boom that would be set off by the leveling of yet another poor, crowded neighborhood to make way for the growing system of boulevards. This was the Paris of ragamuffins calling out their wares and selling herbs from door to door, of milk or ice wagons lumbering through the streets at dawn, of professional photographers, of oyster-eating dandies lounging about in brasseries open to the street, of expensive florists such as Lachaume and Lemaître, of exquisite pastry-makers such as Rebattet and Bourbonneux, of chic cafés such as le café Anglais, le café de la Paix, Weber, and Larue (where Proust as a young adult would often dine, usually alone). This is the Paris in which even the most modest middle-class household kept at least one servant and where ladies were so extravagantly appareled by the first couturiers (Worth, Redfern) that they appeared to be creatures of another species, set apart from ordinary women. This was the Paris that had been enriched by its colonies in the Far East and in Africa; and if it was the condensation of luxury, it was so because it had drained the world dry to pay for its excesses.

This was also the France of heavy, tasteless furniture, of engraved portraits of Prince Eugène, of clocks kept under a glass bell on the mantelpiece, of overstuffed chairs covered with antimacassars and of brass beds warmed by hot-water bottles. Proust lovingly describes (in *Jean Santeuil* and also in the preface to his translation of Ruskin's *Sesame and Lilies*) his aunt Léonie's house in Illiers (her real name was Aunt Elizabeth Amiot). He hovers over the magic lantern in the child's bedroom that cast revolving images from fairy tales on the walls. He lingers over the dining room with its round mahogany table, its walls decorated with old plates, its grandfather clock. In *Swann's Way*, the first volume of *Remembrance of Things Past*, Proust renders his aunt's bedroom in detail: "On one side of her bed were a big yellow chest of drawers in lemon wood and a table that was both dispensary and altar where, below a statuette of the Virgin and a bottle of Vichy water, one discovered prayerbooks and prescriptions for medicine, everything necessary for following from her bed the mass and her cure, to keep the proper times for her pepsin and for vespers."

All his life Proust would remain faithful to the ugly furnishings his parents and relatives had accumulated. The tourist visiting the Musée Carnavalet in Paris today can see his bedroom, preserved down to its last shabby detail: the scarred side table heavily burdened with some of the schoolboy notebooks in which he wrote, the battered Japanese screen behind his bed, a well-worn armchair, and the brass bed itself. The tourist might well agree with Proust's English biographer George Painter, who wrote that "to the end of his life, he filled his room with hideous but sacred objects which spoke to him of his dead parents, his childhood, time lost. He had come into the world not to collect beauty ready-made, but to create it." Proust himself said that since he was too lazy and indifferent to care about his surroundings, "I had the right not to provide nuances to my rooms."

Few incidents about Marcel's childhood are known beyond his terror when grown men (in some versions of the story it's an uncle, in others the curé) pulled him by his curls. In another incident, when he was nine years old, he broke his nose in a fall while playing in the gardens beside the Champs-Elysées. Ten years later his favorite playmates in the gardens were two sisters, Marie and Nelly Benardaky, daughters of the former master of ceremonies of the Russian court. His attachment to Marie (who later married Prince Michel Radziwill) may have been the real-life basis for his fictional first love, Gilberte Swann. Modern readers of the last pages of *Swann's Way*, in which the young narrator falls in love with Gilberte, are often confused about how old these children could be, with their adult-seeming flirtations but also with their silly games of tag and the constant surveillance of them by their nannies. In fact they are teenagers, sixteen or seventeen, in a period before adolescence was invented, at a time when people passed directly from childhood to adulthood, when a boy would be wearing short pants one day and taking a mistress the next.

The presence of these real-life girls in Proust's adolescence and his obvious affection for a few of them call for a clarification. Certainly it would be a mistake to see all of Proust's women as disguised men, even though some of the tomboys in *Remembrance of Things Past* who kick sand at sunbathers on the beach at Balbec or leap over their lounge chairs sound suspiciously unlike the meek, middle-class girls of the day. There has been a lot of discussion about the so-called Albertine strategy—i.e., Proust's disguising an actual affair, say, with his chauffeur, Alfred Agostinelli, as a fictional one with Albertine, a young woman of good family who seems casually lusty and—considering the mores of the time—bizarrely unsupervised.

Proust's gender bending becomes more difficult to decipher when the reader realizes that some of the female characters are unquestionably, quintessentially womanly, such as Odette (despite her lesbian affairs) or the duchesse de Guermantes or the actress Berma (a composite of Sarah Bernhardt and Réjane, two of the big stars of the day, both of whom Proust came to know). Just as clearly, other female characters are unquestionably boys in drag (such as all those delivery "girls" and milk "girls" with whom the Narrator has casual sex). What are we to make of a passage such as this one:

> Of a laundry girl, on a Sunday, there was not the slightest prospect. As for the baker's girl, as ill luck would have it she had rung the bell when Françoise was not about, had left her loaves in their basket on the landing, and had made off. The greengrocer's girl would not call until much later. Once, I had to order a cheese at the dairy, and among the various young female employees had noticed a startling towhead, tall in stature though little more than a child, who seemed to be day-dreaming, amid the other errand-girls, in a distinctly haughty attitude . . .

Sometimes one of these boys-in-drag, such as Albertine, presented as the great love of the Narrator's life, has a "lesbian" affair: The Narrator is depicted as insanely jealous, even to the point of retrospectively, after her death, trying to figure out the identities of Albertine's lesbian partners. Are we to imagine that since Albertine is based on a real-life man, Agostinelli, who was primarily heterosexual, then his/her affairs with women are actually his (Agostinelli's) heterosexual affairs with heterosexual *women?* Many heterosexual men, it seems, at that time did not feel particularly alarmed when their wives had passing affairs with other women; on the contrary, the husbands more often than not were titillated. Can the putatively heterosexual Narrator's overpowering jealousy about Albertine's lesbian affairs actually be a reflection of the homosexual Proust's fury when his bisexual lovers drifted back to women?

In 1881 Marcel had his first asthma crisis as he came back from strolling in the Bois de Boulogne. As he later wrote, "A child who from birth has always breathed without paying any attention has no idea how much the air, which swells so sweetly his chest that he doesn't even notice it, is essential to his life." Proust goes on to say that only if in a fever should the child happen to have a stifling fit would he begin to struggle for his very life.

Asthma was one of the great decisive factors in Proust's development. Because of it he was constantly treated as an invalid (and regarded himself as permanently sickly). Because of it he missed many months of school, was afraid to travel, and constantly had to cancel plans to see friends. Because of it he spent many days in a row, even weeks, lying perfectly still, struggling to breathe. And because of it, at least indirectly, he died an early death at fifty-one. Because of it, too, he was separated from nature, which he worshiped; if he wanted to see hawthorn trees in bloom, he had to be driven through the countryside in a hermetically sealed car. Because of it he was forced to spend much of his life in bed. As the years wore on and his condition worsened, he made only rare sorties outside and then only after midnight, when the dust of the day had settled. Because of it he was forced to embrace solitude, but it also provided him with a ready excuse for keeping people at bay when he wanted to work. Because of it his family and friends and servants were tyrannized by his needs, sometimes even his whims.

It used to be common to ascribe asthma to psychological factors, as though the terrible stifling were symbolic of psychic strangulation or a need for attention. Proust himself sometimes toyed with such explanations, though he reserves his deepest scorn for a doctor in his novel who advises the Narrator's grandmother that her illness, uremia, is all in her head—advice which leads almost immediately to a stroke and her subsequent death. During his life Proust had the lining of his nose cauterized ten times, a painful intervention designed supposedly to make it less susceptible to pollen—all to no avail. Only with the discovery of cortisone, well after Proust's death, did asthmatics win occasional relief. In the 1990s the genetic predisposition to asthma began to be tracked as well as the triggering role of mites in dust, although no cure is yet in sight. But if asthma does not have psychological causes, it has many psychological *consequences*, as Proust's life dramatically proves.

Despite his bouts of asthma, Proust was able to attend school, even if only intermittently. In 1882, a year after his first asthma attack, he entered the Lycée Condorcet, a secondary school known for its glittery student body, including the young Eiffel (whose father's tower would soon be completed), not to mention Jacques Bizet and Daniel Halévy (son and nephew, respectively, of the widow of the dead composer of *Carmen*). When Marcel was seventeen he fell in love with Bizet (Proust called him the "son of Carmen"), who apparently tolerated his attentions for a while but soon rejected him altogether. Daniel Halévy later recalled about Proust, "There was something about him which we found unpleasant. His kindnesses and tender attentions seemed mere mannerisms and poses, and we took occasion to tell him so to his face. Poor, unhappy boy, we were beastly to him." Halévy saw him "with his huge oriental eyes, his big white collar and flying cravat, as a sort of disturbed and disturbing archangel." Proust's mother suspected that her son and Bizet were lovers and forbade Marcel to spend time alone with the boy. Marcel was furious. He threatened to spend all his time with Bizet outside their homes ("I'll turn a café into a house for both of us"). He wrote Bizet about the enforced rupture: "Why? You see, I know nothing about it. And for how long? Perhaps forever, perhaps for a few days. Why? . . . Perhaps she worries for my sake about this affection that is a bit excessive, don't you think? and which could degenerate (she may think this) into . . . a sensual affection . . . perhaps because she supposes that in general you have the same faults as I (a rebellious mind, a confused mind; perhaps even onanism). . . ." When Bizet rejected Marcel's sexual advances, Marcel wrote him, "Perhaps you're right. However I find it's always sad not to pluck the delicious flower that soon we'll no longer be able to gather. For then it will have become the forbidden fruit."

Apparently Marcel believed that sex between boys was innocent and became a "vice" only with age. He tried to clarify this argument in a letter to Bizet's friend Halévy (whom he was also pursuing), in which he wrote that there are young men (he intimated he might be one) who love one another, cannot bear to be apart, seat their partner on their knees, who love each other for their flesh and call each other "darling," who write each other passionate love letters— "and yet for nothing in the world would perform pederasty. However, love generally carries them away and they masturbate each other. In short, they are lovers. And I don't know why their love is more unclean than the usual sort of love." One wonders what Proust thought the word *pédérastie* might mean (it's the usual French word for "homosexuality," although Proust later came to prefer *inversion*). In writing a self-portrait for Robert Dreyfus, yet another school friend in the same tight little circle, Proust described himself as someone who "under the pretext of loving a friend as a father, might actually love him as a woman would." A tragic coincidence would have it that the little Bizet, Proust's first love, would become a drug addict and, later, would commit suicide just ten days before Proust himself would die.

After being disappointed in love with Bizet, Proust transferred all his attentions to Bizet's mother, Geneviève, who was born Halévy. Her father, Fromental Halévy, had composed the opera *La Juive*, which Proust refers to more than once in *Remembrance of Things Past*. Her uncle and cousin wrote the libretto for many operas and operettas, including *Carmen*. Her first husband was Bizet; ten years after his death at thirty-eight, she married a rich man named Emile Straus, the Rothschilds' lawyer and a major collector of Monet's paintings. Madame Straus became Proust's model for wit. It was she who, when she accompanied her former music teacher, Gounod, to an opera and he remarked that they'd just heard a passage that was "perfectly octagonal," exclaimed, "Oh, I was just about to say the same myself!" And it was she who, while attending an "intellectual" dinner where everyone was supposed to give an opinion on adultery, said airily—and impertinently— "I'm so sorry, I prepared incest by mistake." After Dreyfus was at last liberated, following years of national controversy, he was introduced to Madame Straus, who said, "I've heard a lot about you." When Proust would later come to create one of his most memorable characters, the duchesse de Guermantes, he would base her wit on Madame Straus's.

Although at first Proust pretended to be in love with her

(which her vanity required of all her male admirers), he soon enough settled into a friendship with her that was perhaps the most enduring and nourishing of his life. His correspondence with her is one of the most sustained—and the one in which he divulges the most information about his all-important artistic plans, even his love life. If he was seldom disinterested in his pursuit of men (who were all too often heterosexual and incapable of returning his affection in the form he longed for), in an older woman of Madame Straus's intelligence and loyalty he found a kindred spirit. Proust himself was aware of this phenomenon; in speaking of one of his characters, Robert de Saint-Loup, who has just "come out" and turned gay, the Narrator writes that he had also turned cold to his male companions, "since men, now that they were capable of arousing his desires, could no longer inspire his friendship."

III

―――――

BUT NOT ALL of Proust's energies as an adolescent went into seduction. The curriculum at the Lycée Condorcet was thorough and challenging, and Proust received an excellent introduction there to Greek, Latin, French, the natural sciences, and philosophy. If he was never head of the class, neither was he ever the last—despite his frequent absences, his nervousness (he was constantly excusing himself to go to the toilet), and his distractibility (he was always passing notes to classmates or making jokes during botanical field trips). He was already being teased for his long sentences, far-fetched comparisons, and overexuberant eloquence.

His favorite professor was Alphonse Darlu, a philosopher who believed in spirituality but not Christianity (he was a follower of Tolstoy). At a time when most French thinkers remained positivists and espoused science, progress and empiricism, Darlu embraced metaphysics, idealism, and a cult of truthfulness. Proust called him in the dedication of one book the master who had most influenced his thought. Once Proust's idealism is noticed it seems to appear in nearly every line of his great novel. For instance, at the end of *Swann's Way* the Narrator, in love with Swann's daughter Gilberte, goes in search of her in the park beside the Champs-Elysées. There he finds her at play. She suddenly throws him a ball, and, as Proust writes, "Like the idealist philosopher whose body takes account of the external world in the reality of which his intellect declines to believe, the same self which had made me greet her before I had identified her now urged me to seize the ball that she handed to me (as though she were a companion with whom I had come to play, and not a sister-soul with whom I had come to be united). . . ." Proust rejected André Gide's more ordinary form of realism, his method of building up a character or situation through the accretion of small details, by saying that he, Proust, could be interested only in those details that pointed towards a general truth or that expressed poetic enchantment. Every page of Proust's masterpiece piles up several "general truths" and adds to the elevated, philosophical tone. Perhaps because of this tone Proust could get away with writing about even the most scandalous subjects without ruffling his readers.

An undoctrinaire spirituality, learned from Professor Darlu, remained with Proust his whole life and informs nearly every page of his massive book. He may seldom write about God, but the natural reflex of his mind is to move from the concrete particular to the abstract principle. As he wrote a friend in 1915: "If I have no religion . . . on the other hand a religious preoccupation has never been absent for a single day from my life." He mentions that he has just assured a grieving father that someday he may see his dead son again, but then Proust adds, "Yet the more one is religious the less one dares to move towards certainty, to go beyond what one actually believes; I don't deny anything, I believe in the possibility of everything, while objections based on the existence of Evil, etc. strike me as absurd, since Suffering alone seems to me to have made (and to continue to make) Man a bit more than a brute. But to go from that on to certainty, even to Hope, is a long journey. I haven't yet crossed that threshold—will I ever?"

If, as Camus once observed, Americans are the only novelists who don't think they need to be intellectuals, one could add that European novelists are, on the contrary, those that consider themselves most under an obligation to develop a philosophy. What is certain is that Proust is the great philosophical novelist, rivaled only by George Eliot (whom he admired intensely) and, in this century, a trio of German-speaking writers he did not live long enough to read—Thomas Mann, Hermann Broch, and Robert Musil. Proust certainly thought of himself as a thinker and he once wrote a friend: "I very much wish to finish the work I've begun and to put in it those truths that I know will be nourished by it and that otherwise will be destroyed with me." But if he was a philosopher, at the same time he had more faith in the senses and in memory than in the intellect to experience ultimate truths.

In 1886 the fifteen-year-old Proust responded to a questionnaire in English that one of his girlfriends had found printed in an album of the period. He listed his favorite composers as Mozart and Gounod (the composer of *Faust*). His idea of happiness: "To live near all those whom I love with the charms of nature, a quantity of books and musical scores, and not far from a French theater." "To be separated from Mama" was his idea of unhappiness and "the private life of geniuses" was the fault he was most ready to forgive. That same year he paid his last visit to Illiers in the autumn; his asthma no longer permitted him to go to the countryside, but the town, his aunt's garden, the church, her neighbors and her cook, the smell of orrisroot in the toilet where years before he had felt his first sexual stirrings—all would be preserved perfectly in the clear amber of his extraordinary memory.

By 1888, when he was seventeen, Proust was struggling to overcome his homosexual urges. He wrote to Daniel Halévy, "Don't treat me as a pederast, that wounds me. Morally I'm trying, if only out of a sense of elegance, to remain pure."

Simultaneously he began to pay court to Laure Hayman, his uncle's (and, as it turned out, his father's) mistress, who would become the model of his most convincing female character, Odette, the "grande cocotte" whom Charles Swann loves and eventually marries. Only after Dr. Proust's death did Marcel discover that his father had been more than just a friend to Laure Hayman; the discovery wasn't a shock, since Dr. Proust had always held Laure up as the very standard of elegance, tact, and beauty. Marcel, too, paid her elaborate (if entirely sexless) court and once absurdly declared that "we live in the century of Laure Hayman." In real life Laure had had an exotic background (she was born on a ranch in the Andes) and was a descendant of the English painter Francis Hayman—a founder of the Royal Academy and Gainsborough's teacher. She'd been the lover, successively, of the duc d'Orléans; the king of Greece; Karageorgević, pretender to the Serbian throne; Prince Karl Egon von Fürstenberg; the banker Bischoffsheim—and a handsome young secretary at the British embassy. She had a house on the same street where Proust placed Odette, the rue La Pérouse, a stone's throw from the Arc de Triomphe.

Like Léa in Colette's *Chéri*, Laure was approaching forty when she first met Proust, who was seventeen. Like Léa, she had secured her fortune through love, owned extraordinary pearls, was both practical and romantic. But whereas Chéri becomes the pampered lover of Léa, a woman his mother's age, Proust was just another bauble that Laure added to her china collection (she called him "my little porcelain psychologist"). Like Odette in *Remembrance of Things Past*, she strolled often in the Bois de Boulogne or rode horseback there. Like Odette, she loved chrysanthemums (which Proust offered her in profusion, though he could ill afford them on his allowance, and she even reported to Proust's father that his son was becoming too extravagant). Unlike Odette, whom the Narrator's mother is too prudish and respectable to meet, the real Laure Hayman was frequently invited to dinner at Dr. and Mrs. Proust's.

During his last year at the Lycée de Condorcet Proust published with his school friends two literary magazines, first *La Revue Verte*, then *La Revue Lilas* (green and lilac seem the perfect fin-de-siècle colors). In *The Lilac Review* the seventeen-year-old boy would publish a story about an ancient Greek named Glaukos: "Today his heart is calm. But he has many friends and he is infinitely loved by certain of them. . . . Often he is seated on the nervous knees of one of his friends, cheek to cheek, body to body, and he discusses with him Aristotle's philosophy and Euripides' poems, while the two of them kiss and caress each other and say elegant and wise things."

In making harsh marginal comments on a poem by Daniel Halévy, Proust revealed that he was indifferent to the taste of his friends for the decadent writers of the day and that he preferred the classics—and absolute sincerity above all literary posing. Already at age seventeen he'd made fidelity to truth his artistic standard par excellence. Later he would write an essay attacking obscurity in literature. This truth telling—joined to his long sentences, his many comparisons, his resolution to mine every last ounce of gold from a subject—is what made his writing seem old-fashioned to his contemporaries and renders it eternally fresh to us. Most of the good writers of Proust's generation, such as André Gide and Paul Claudel, were almost minimalists. But later generations are not sensitive to such fads, no more than are modern listeners bothered by the fact that Bach sounded tiresomely polyphonic and dated to his contemporaries.

After graduation Proust signed up on November 11, 1889, for a year of military service (by volunteering for one year he avoided being enlisted for three years of service). Four days later he was stationed in Orléans. In one of the photos of him from the period, he is walking with his fists clenched, his eyes burning under a military shako two sizes too big for him, his mouth outlined with a black mustache and a dab of goatee, his skinny body shrouded in a belted greatcoat. Although fifteen years later he would recall his year as a soldier with total delight, as "a paradise," at the time he complained bitterly and his mother had to write him consoling, babying letters, telling him to think of the twelve months as twelve chocolate squares. . . .

In *The Guermantes Way* the "paradisal" side of military life is shown in the long chapter about Doncières (Orléans), where the Narrator pays a visit to the dashing young Dreyfusard and democratic aristocrat Robert de Saint-Loup. Every autobiographical novel inevitably mixes harsh truths about its first-person hero with a bit of wish fulfillment. In this military chapter the element of wish fulfillment becomes almost embarrassingly overwhelming. Not only is

Saint-Loup thrilled that the Narrator has condescended to visit him, but all his fellow officers are equally impressed by the Narrator's brilliant conversation. Ostensibly the Narrator, who has convinced himself he is in love with the duchesse de Guermantes (a haughty aristocrat of his mother's age with whom he has never exchanged a word), comes to Doncières to persuade her nephew, Saint-Loup, to arrange an introduction to the aunt. But this mission seems to be just an excuse for the Narrator to enjoy the company of all these adoring men, who treat him as though he's a delightful mascot—a genius but also a lovable child.

Civilians are forbidden to stay in the barracks with the soldiers, and Saint-Loup has found a hotel room for the Narrator. But when he realizes that the Narrator will pass a sleepless night all alone, he gets the rules bent. When Saint-Loup asks the Narrator if he'd rather spend the night with him, the Narrator replies:

> "Oh, Robert, it's cruel of you to be sarcastic about it, . . . You know it's not possible, and you know how wretched I shall be over there."
>
> "Well, you flatter me!" he replied. "Because it actually occurred to me that you'd rather stay here tonight. And that is precisely what I went to ask the Captain."
>
> "And he has given you leave?" I cried.
>
> "He hadn't the slightest objection."
>
> "Oh! I adore him."
>
> "No, that would be going too far. But now, let me just

get hold of my batman and tell him to see about our dinner," he went on, while I turned away to hide my tears.

This scene scarcely reeks of military stoicism and seems highly implausible, but it is no doubt an accurate picture of how Proust wished his straight male friends would treat him. No wonder he would so often be disappointed in friendship.

In January 1890 his maternal grandmother died. The following fall, after his military service was over, Proust signed up to read law in Paris and to study politics at the famous "Sciences-Po," the nickname for the Ecole libre des sciences politiques, a university comparable in prestige to Oxford or Harvard. He spent September at Cabourg, an elegant resort on the Norman coast that he later made famous under the name of Balbec. It is here that the Narrator in *Sodom and Gomorrah*, exhausted by the five-hour train trip from Paris, suddenly remembers that his grandmother had helped him untie his shoes once under similar circumstances—and he dissolves in sobs, able at last to grieve over her death:

> I had just perceived, in my memory, stooping over with fatigue, the tender, preoccupied, disappointed face of my grandmother, as she had been on that first evening of our arrival, the face not of that grandmother whom I had been astonished and remorseful at having so little missed, and who had nothing in common with her save her name,

but of my real grandmother, of whom, for the first time since the afternoon of her stroke in the Champs Elysées, I now recaptured the living reality in a complete and involuntary memory.

Proust develops here the idea that our memory is not like a vase in which all the contents—all the things that we have felt in the past—are available simultaneously. No, the heart has its intermittencies, and memories come flooding back to us in their full, sensuous force only when triggered involuntarily by tastes or smells or other sensations over which we have no control. This idea of involuntary memory would become one of the touchstones of *Remembrance of Things Past* and one of his chief principles of literary architecture.

Proust's three years as a law student and especially at the Ecole libre des sciences politiques gave him an access not only to the realities covered by these subjects but, more important for a writer, to their *vocabularies,* including their sophisticated strategies of evasiveness. It is tempting to reduce Proust to an invalid and a snob who is fascinated only by his own health and his ascent up the social ladder, but such a caricature leaves out the immensity of his social canvas. Proust's chief inspiration as a novelist was the omnivorous Balzac, and like his great predecessor, Proust could enter the world of the army or the diplomatic corps as easily as he could render an aristocratic salon or a male bordello or the confines of his own cork-lined bedroom.

At Sciences-Po he took a course in diplomacy from the famous Albert Sorel, who became the main model for Monsieur de Norpois, the ultimate slippery statesman, the sort of character that writers who themselves were diplomats and who knew the milieu better than Proust (Stendhal, Chateaubriand, and Gobineau, among others) never succeeded in depicting with equal verve. In a celebrated scene in *The Guermantes Way* Bloch, a Jew and Dreyfusard, tries to corner the ex-ambassador Norpois about where he (and the government) stand with respect to the Dreyfus case. For a dozen pages Norpois skillfully dodges the question by secreting a cloud of murky verbiage. In a passing remark, the Narrator speculates that Norpois may be so indirect because "the maxims of his political wisdom being applicable only to questions of form, of procedure, of expediency, they were as powerless to solve questions of fact as, in philosophy, pure logic is powerless to tackle the problems of existence. . . ."

While he was at Sciences-Po Proust began his extraordinary conquest of aristocratic and artistic Paris. In 1891 he met Oscar Wilde, who at the time was at the height of his fame, witty, the sensation of Mallarmé's salon, voluble in French, even capable of writing a play in the language (*Salomé*, which later became the text of Richard Strauss's opera). Apparently Proust, just twenty, invited the powdered, perfumed, puffy Irish giant to his family's apartment for dinner but Wilde, after taking a single glance at the heavy, dark furniture, said, "How ugly everything is here," and left. Even if the encounter was brief (or even apocryphal), Wilde's subsequent trial and condemnation for homosexuality marked Proust, who, when he came to write about "the race of queens" in *Sodom and Gomorrah*, alluded to Wilde's tragic fall with little sympathy yet with full cognizance of its historic significance.

Almost equally definitive for gay men of Proust's epoch was the case of Prince Philip von Eulenburg (1847–1921), a former ambassador to Vienna and an intimate friend of Kaiser Wilhelm II of Germany. Eulenburg was accused of homosexuality in 1906. A bellicose German journalist who disliked the Kaiser's pacifist circle brought the morals charge against him, and the Kaiser instantly handed his tainted friend over to the wolves. Several subsequent trials failed to clear Eulenburg's name, despite the fact that he was the father of nine children. Proust himself dated the introduction of the term "homosexuality" into the French language from the time of this scandal, although as a medical term it had existed in German since 1869, when it had first been introduced by a Hungarian doctor; previously the usual term in France had been *inverti* ("invert"), or to use Balzac's slangier word, *tante* (literally "auntie," the equivalent to "queen" in English).

Proust was also meeting gifted French homosexuals of his own age. In fact, in 1892 he had his photo taken with Robert de Flers, the future marquis de Flers and the author of successful comedies and libretti for operettas, and Lucien Daudet, the son of the (then) celebrated writer Alphonse

Daudet (*Letters from My Windmill* and *Sapho*). The young Lucien would later become the unofficial gentleman-in-waiting to the ex-empress Eugénie, who had outlived her husband, Napoleon III, and her son, the prince imperial, killed in Africa. The Spanish-born empress had at first been exiled to England after her husband lost the French throne in 1871, but later she was permitted to live in Biarritz, the French Atlantic coastal resort close to the Spanish border, and there she held a mournful shadow court until her death in the 1920s. Her most faithful attendant was the ardent Lucien, who wrote several books about her.

If Madame Proust had had any doubts about her son's homosexuality, they were quickly banished when she saw the photo of Proust, carefully groomed and seated, a flower in his buttonhole, flanked on one side by the standing Flers, with his flowing bohemian silk cravat, and on the other by the affected Lucien, a hand resting on Marcel's shoulder, the other hand suspended in the air as though he had just plucked an invisible harp string. All three young men have wispy mustaches and tightly buttoned jackets. Lucien is gazing down at Marcel with devoted rapture. Edmond de Goncourt described Lucien as "a handsome young man, curled, well-dressed, pomaded, painted and powdered" with "a tiny vest-pocket voice." Even Lucien's father, Alphonse, thought he was a bit too chic. The quarrel between Proust and his parents reported in *Jean Santeuil* which ended with the young hero breaking a Venetian vase was in reality prompted by Madame Proust's horror at the photo, which she forbade her son to circulate. Apparently Madame Proust also objected to Lucien's powdered face and the garish color of his tie, since Marcel dashed off a letter: "I don't think there's any harm in being photographed with Robert de Flers and if Lucien Daudet is wearing a tie a little too bright or a complexion a bit too pale, that's a problem that disappears in the photograph which doesn't render colors." In a second letter, written at midnight on November 4, 1896, and slipped under his mother's door, Proust accedes to her demands and writes: "The best would be if I'm the one to take all the proofs, I'll give one to each of them and I'll hand over the rest to you: in that way they won't be in circulation (since you find in all this something I fail to understand)."

At the same time that Proust was eager to make love to other young men, he was equally determined to avoid the label "homosexual." Years later he would tell André Gide that one could write about homosexuality even at great length, so long as one did not ascribe it to oneself. This bit of literary advice is coherent with Proust's general closetedness—a secretiveness that was all the more absurd since everyone near him knew he was gay.

IV

PROUST WAS BEGINNING to rise in society, which slightly dismayed (and secretly thrilled) his staid parents, who were shocked to discover around their dining table dukes and duchesses, painters in vogue and well-known actresses. Even though he was opposed to note-taking and direct observation from life, Proust revealed already at this early date his capacity for screamingly funny imitations of his new acquaintances (a vaudevillian talent that would come in handy later when he would begin to create his cast of great Dickensian eccentrics: the baron de Charlus, Madame Verdurin, the duc de Guermantes, the maid Françoise, all of whom have a distinctive, not to say preposterous, way of speaking).

This verbal miming had its counterpart in Proust's love of writing pastiches, which he considered a kind of "criticism in action" (when he was feeling positive) and an "imbecile exercise" (when he was fed up with his addiction to this form). To write "in the manner of" a famous novelist or essayist of the past was something that Proust mastered early and continued to do all his life. He even published a volume containing his pastiches. He avoided writers such as Mérimée and Voltaire, since a simple, straightforward style like theirs was difficult to parody (just as drag queens avoid "doing" unadorned beauties such as Audrey Hepburn and are inspired by highly constructed women such as Mae West or Barbra Streisand). Proust also enjoyed imitating writers whose style he admired excessively (such as Balzac and Flaubert) so that he could be in conscious control of their influence on him and, in a sense, "exorcise" their impact on his prose. As he put it, "Do a voluntary pastiche in order to become original again afterwards and not produce involuntary pastiches the rest of one's life." Much later, after writing his pastiche of Flaubert, Proust composed a critical essay on the same master, explaining: "Our mind is never satisfied if it has not been able to give a clear analysis of what it first unconsciously produced, or a living recreation of what it had first patiently analyzed."

Proust was not just an irritating imitator. He must have had a wonderfully ingratiating personality as well, since long before he began to publish fiction of lasting importance he was already able to attract some of the most sought-after people of his day, including the writers Anatole France and Maurice Barrès. In his early twenties he became a member of Princess Mathilde's salon. She was Napoleon's niece, an old lady who'd survived an unhappy marriage to the psychopathic Prince Demidov, nephew of Czar Nicholas I, and who had outlived the members of her brilliant literary coterie, which had included Dumas *fils,* author of *La Dame aux camélias,* on which the opera *La Traviata* is based; Flaubert, who may have been her lover; Mérimée, author of the story from which the opera *Carmen* is drawn; the historian Taine; the critic Sainte-Beuve, whose ideas Proust would devote several years to demolishing; and the outstanding diarists of the nineteenth century, the Goncourt brothers, Edmond and Jules. By the time Proust came along, only Edmond de Goncourt was still alive (in *Remembrance of Things Past* Proust creates a pastiche of the Goncourt journal). But Proust was so excited at meeting Princess Mathilde, who represented a conjunction of literary and dynastic legends, that he later made her a character in his novel under her own name.

People often say, casually and not altogether accurately, that Proust's thinking was deeply affected by his encounter at this time with the most influential French philosopher of the turn of the century, Henri Bergson, who in 1892 married Proust's cousin Louise Neuburger. But in fact the two men never had a serious conversation except once, after World War I, when they discussed the nature of sleep, a debate that gets replayed in *Sodom and Gomorrah.* Bergson subscribed to ideas similar to Freud's, that the function of dreams is to explain away inner conflicts and external stimuli (noises, drafts, disagreeable thoughts) that might trouble a peaceful sleep, whereas Proust saw dreaming as its own province, with its own system of time, and for him the challenge in awakening was precisely how to insert sleep's time system into the utterly different system of time used when awake. They also disagreed about the effect of narcotics on memory. Bergson admitted of no effect, whereas Proust thought that higher thoughts (philosophical ideas, for instance) might not be erased, but thoughts about everyday maneuverings (the necessity to respond to an invitation, for instance) could be wiped out entirely. In any event, the two men had many other parallel concerns (about the basic animating spirit governing the world; time; laughter; and the perception of space and memory), but Bergson seems to have dismissed Proust as someone interested only in high society (*le monde*).

Again and again Proust would suffer from his reputation as a socialite, a *mondain*. It was certainly true that most of his friends as a young adult (and there were dozens of them) were rich or titled or talented or all three, and that very few belonged to the social milieu into which he had been born. And it was certainly true he gave the impression of being snobbish. Jean Cocteau wrote, "Proust doesn't hesitate to judge society people and accuse them of stupidity. He finds them stupid but superior, which is the very definition of snobbism." But, as Proust's writings demonstrate, when he was young and naive a noble name was for him a piece of living, breathing, walking, talking history, a modern incarnation of a medieval legend. The first time the Narrator sees the duchesse de Guermantes, for instance, she is kneeling in the local Combray church in the chapel of Gilbert the Bad, reserved for members of her family: "My disappointment was immense. It arose from my not having borne in mind, when I thought of Madame de Guermantes, that I was picturing her to myself in the colours of a tapestry or a stained-glass window, as living in another century, as being of another substance than the rest of the human race. Never had it occurred to me that she might have a red face, a mauve scarf like Madame Sazerat. . . ." Later, when he is no longer so fascinated by her, he comes to enjoy her way of conversing, by turns earthy and refined, witty and ceremonial—a true reliquary of authentic French. And the Narrator is never able to rid himself entirely of his poetic, heraldic appreciation of the lady: "I knew quite well that to a number of intelligent people she was merely a lady like any other, the name duchesse de Guermantes signifying nothing, now that there are no longer any duchies or principalities; but I had adopted a different point of view in my manner of enjoying people and places. This lady in furs braving the bad weather seemed to me to carry with her all the castles of the territories of which she was duchess, princess, viscountess, as the figures carved over a portal hold in their hands the cathedral they have built or the city they have defended."

Certainly Proust may have started out as a snob, but he ended up as the most penetrating critic of snobbism who ever lived. He showed how empty are its victories, how evanescent its conquests. More particularly, he demonstrated the vanity and cruelty and insecurity and affectedness—and snobbishness!—of even the most sought-after members of society. Many of the originals for his characters recognized how damning his portraits were. The comtesse de Chévigné, one of the models for the duchesse de Guermantes, was so furious when she skimmed *The Guermantes Way* that she broke off twenty-five years' worth of friendship and burned Proust's many letters; to destroy a writer's writing is surely the most wounding revenge.

The society painter Jacques-Emile Blanche, for whom Proust posed in 1892, has left us an equally unforgettable verbal portrait of someone who as a youngster would frighten his playmates by seizing them by the hand and announcing his need to possess them with all the force of a tyrant: "Already he pretended to attribute sublime virtues to one friend or another, although in his deepest heart he judged people at their true value. A Proust can only be someone isolated—is that the price genius must pay? We feel we must keep such an observer, such an implacable judge, at a distance, as though he were a large, hot brazier."

Curiously, this deadly clear evaluation of other people was disguised by his elaborate politeness—addressed even to servants (unusual for the period, when most people were contemptuous of the social classes below them). Proust's complicated way of talking was dubbed by his friends with the French made-up verb *proustifier*, "to Proustify." Proust was quite capable of waking up in the middle of the night to worry that when Madame Straus's husband had complained of a young man who never rose from his chair when older people entered the room he'd meant to reproach Proust for the same rudeness, despite the fact that he was clearly too ill to stand up repeatedly and was by that point an old friend of the family. Questions of etiquette and deeper matters of genuine kindness and respect haunted Proust all his life. Nevertheless, he could not tolerate polite clichés, which he and his friend Lucien Daudet termed *louchonneries*, by which they meant "expressions that make you cross your eyes"—e.g., falsely elegant variations such as "Albion" for England and "Green Erin" for Ireland, or obviously hypocritical expressions such as "those fine folks" (*les braves gens*) applied by aristocrats to peasants.

When he was twenty-one he responded to a second questionnaire (this one in French, printed in a friend's album, something like a yearbook today), in which this time he identified as his principal trait "the need to be loved or, more precisely, the need to be caressed and spoiled rather than the need to be admired." He sought in a man "feminine charms" and in a woman "masculine virtues." His main fault was not wanting to know things and not being able to will himself into action—he lacked willpower.

According to the questionnaire, his favorite writers now included two living masters, Pierre Loti and Anatole France. Loti was an absurd member of the navy and the French Academy who loved to dress up (as a pharaoh, an Arab chieftain, a Japanese warlord) and whose house on the Atlantic coast in Rochefort was part Muslim mosque, part Turkish corner, and part medieval fortress. His novels were equally exotic: *The Disenchanted*, about the plight of modern Turkish women; *To Morocco*, about an overland trip in springtime from Tangier to Fez; and *Madame Chrysanthème*, about a Japanese geisha abandoned by a French naval officer. Anatole France, whom Proust knew well and who was a far more considerable novelist than Loti (France won the Nobel Prize), wrote *The Red Lily*, a psychological novel of great delicacy about adultery among artistically inclined French aristocrats on a trip to Florence, a book that lacks only amplitude and force to be a masterpiece on a level with *Madame Bovary*. It inspired Proust with its subtle psychology, its refined sensuality, its portrait of a poet much like Verlaine.

Anatole France's work moved him with its tone of muted melancholy, gentle pessimism, and convinced solipsism. France's classical style—straightforward and always lucid—steered Proust away from the deliberate obscurantism of symbolist poets and prose writers, just as Proust's later discovery of the exalted Ruskin would influence him to abandon France's materialism for a more congenial brand of spiritualism, one that Proust's education had in any event predisposed him to embrace.

To be sure, neither Loti nor France was a writer as ambitious or as gifted as the earlier nineteenth-century masters Balzac, Stendhal, and Flaubert. Proust lived in a period of inferior writers but of a superior culture. If Paris for the moment was a city without great authors, it had plenty of great readers, connoisseurs alert to true achievement in the arts. More important for a social novelist (and weren't almost all novels about society?), Proust half-belonged to a gossipy, cultivated, leisurely world. He knew all the secrets of the aristocracy and spent thirty years learning their rituals, feuds, genealogies, and vanities, but he was also distanced from this world by the fact he was half-Jewish, untitled, gay, and an invalid. It was this distance, of course, which made him such an acute observer. As he once remarked, people of action (and socialites are, in their small way, people of action) are always too busy preparing for the next event to remember the past.

The present princesse de Caraman-Chimay once told me that when Proust died, her great-uncle Comte Henri Greffulhe (the main model for the duc de Guermantes), found his butler sobbing. "But why are you grieving? Did you know Monsieur Proust?" "Oh, yes," the butler replied, "every time there would be a ball here, Monsieur Proust would come by the next day and quiz me about who had come, what they said, how they were related to one another and so on. Such a nice man—and he always left such a generous tip!" Proust's relationship to society is encapsulated in this story—the indirect information gleaned from a knowledgeable and observant butler, the kindness to servants, the prizing and preserving of anecdotes which the hosts themselves quickly forget . . . even the big tip.

Proust began with *Remembrance of Things Past* one of the major trends of the century—to confound autobiography and fiction—yet the originality of his formal innovations was not immediately apparent to his contemporaries because his work was rooted in the aristocratic past, and because his style was not lean, oblique, modern, pregnant with omissions and silence, but rather a fully saturated style, reminiscent of no writer in the French past except the seventeenth-century diarist the duc de Saint-Simon, one of Louis XIV's disgruntled courtiers, a gifted gossip and a master at word portraits. If the world of aristocratic salons provided Proust with his most compelling subject matter, that same subject alienated many of his potential readers. After he became famous—and especially after his death— many of the serious intellectuals and artists who'd dismissed him earlier as a hanger-on, a society parasite, a gossip columnist (for Proust wrote accounts of salons for the news-paper *Le Figaro*) suddenly had to scratch their heads and re-evaluate him. Perhaps because he was known to be gay (at least to an inner circle), his contemporaries couldn't imagine that such a popinjay could turn out to be the greatest novelist of the new century.

V

In 1892 AND 1893 PROUST, who was in his early twenties, and four of his friends (including Daniel Halévy, Robert Dreyfus, and Fernand Gregh) founded a literary magazine called *Le Banquet* (the French name for Plato's *Symposium*). In it Proust published critical articles and short stories that he would later collect in his first published book, *Pleasures and Days*. (The title is a frivolous variation on the sober title of another ancient Greek classic, Hesiod's *Works and Days*.) When *Le Banquet* folded in 1893, Proust began to publish fiction in *La Revue Blanche*, including a sketch, "Before the Night," the confession of a lesbian: "It is no less moral—or rather not more immoral—that a woman should find pleasure with another woman rather than with a being of the opposite sex." Elsewhere, the female speaker asks, "How can we be indignant about habits that Socrates (he was referring to men, but isn't it the same thing), he who drank hemlock rather than commit an injustice, cheerfully approved in his favorite male friends?"

Fernand Gregh, his co-editor on *Le Banquet*, left an

intriguing evaluation of Proust at this time. Gregh wrote that Proust was so determined to be loved he was willing to risk being scorned; he was handsome, especially when he spoke and his eyes glowed; he appeared to be passive but he was really active: "He creates the impression of giving, and he takes."

In 1893 Proust met Robert de Montesquiou at the house of the hostess-painter Madeleine Lemaire, of whom the younger Dumas said she had created more roses than God. (Proust, the flatterer, went Dumas one better by starting a sonnet to Madame Lemaire with these words: "You do more than God—an eternal springtime.") Montesquiou—a monster of egotism who needed constant praise as exaggerated as that which Nero had required, and who could be as sadistic as the Roman emperor if it was not forthcoming—was thirty-seven when Proust, just twenty-two years old, met him. In 1909 he gave a hint of his pretensions when he answered a questionnaire ("Who are you?") by saying: "Related to a large part of the European aristocracy. Ancestors: Field-Marshals: Blaise de Montluc, Jean de Gassion, Pierre de Montesquiou, Anne-Pierre de Montesquiou, the conqueror of Savoy, d'Artagnan (the hero of *The Three Musketeers*), the abbot de Montesquiou, Louis XVIII's minister, the General Count A. de Montesquiou, Napoleon's aide-de-camp." Proust admired this dandy with his leanness ("I look like a greyhound in a greatcoat," he said of himself), his fabled friendships with legendary poets such as Verlaine and Mallarmé, and his cult of the beautiful conducted in his extravagant house, the Rose Pavilion. He had served as the model for the total aesthete des Esseintes in Huysmans's novel *Against the Grain*, in which an aristocrat never stirs from his house, where he has created a sumptuous, totally artificial interior that evokes in each room a different epoch or climate. Des Esseintes never knows the hour of the day outside, since the lighting in his rooms is constant, and even the scents are controlled; to bring out the colors in his carpets he has studded with jewels the back of a giant sea turtle that is meant to lumber over the kilims— except the creature dies and begins to rot.

A bejeweled, rotting turtle was a good emblem for the new school of poets and novelists, the decadents, writers who celebrated death, sexual excess, and a withdrawal from the world. To be sure, Huysmans had never met Montesquiou or visited his apartments on the quai d'Orsay, but Mallarmé had given Huysmans a full report of his visit, and a gilded turtle certainly did occupy the premises, and the real Montesquiou did have a winter room decorated with polar-bear rugs, a sleigh, and mica-flake snow. Montesquiou was a *grand seigneur*, distinguished by such overweening pride that a society painter was once overheard saying about him, "There's one good thing about the French Revolution. If it hadn't happened, that man would have had us beating his ponds to keep the frogs quiet."

In his high-pitched, grating voice Montesquiou was constantly reciting his own poetry from volumes with names like *Hydrangeas*, *The Bats*, and *The Red Beads*, or presiding over literary and musical soirées. No praise was too extravagant, and Proust knew how to lay it on thick. "You are the sovereign not only of transitory, but of eternal things," Proust wrote him. On another occasion Proust (ridiculously) compared him to the seventeenth-century playwright Corneille, the father of French classical theater. But Proust was also the master of the *nuanced* compliment; after Montesquiou showed him his celebrated Japanese dwarf trees, Proust had the nerve to write him that his soul was "a garden as rare and fastidious as the one in which you allowed me to walk the other day. . . ." And Montesquiou heard that Proust kept his friends in stitches imitating his way of speaking, of laughing, and of stamping his foot. Most daring of all, Proust proposed to write an essay to be titled "The Simplicity of Monsieur Montesquiou," who had never been previously accused of such a quality.

But Proust was impressed by Montesquiou's combination of reverence for the arts and extraordinary social connections; the young man shared the first and coveted the second. As a literary duchess, Elizabeth de Clermont-Tonnerre, wrote in her 1925 study, *Robert de Montesquiou et Marcel Proust:* "And then there are the endless tales, the flashing conversations, the magnificent stories. Montesquiou empties out his closets, hands over all his secrets. He talks, he talks, he unpacks his anecdotes, witticisms, characteristics. He dazzles Proust with sumptuous parades."

Proust was much later to base his most memorable character, the baron de Charlus, on Montesquiou—on his tantrums, his preposterous pride in his social position and lineage, his endless monologues. To be sure, the baron's bulky body and rouged cheeks were reminiscent more of the baron Jacques Doasan, who ruined himself heaping presents on a Polish violinist (just as Charlus ruins himself over the French violinist Charles Morel). Doasan also provided Charlus with his malicious tongue; once when a well-meaning acquaintance entreated him to give up his gossiping, Doasan replied coolly, "It can't be helped, I prefer my vices to my friends." And of course Proust assigned some of his own tyrannical whims, his aestheticizing, and his peevishness to Charlus, for Proust was capable of seeing himself in a satirical light and was always the first to get the joke. In his dealings with the prickly Montesquiou, however, Proust alternated between slavish fawning and stinging satire.

In 1894, when Proust was twenty-three, he met the composer Reynaldo Hahn, with whom he would have a passionate and (given the period) surprisingly open affair for the next two years. Hahn was just eighteen years old. Thanks to Hahn, Proust plunged into the world of music; his writing soon betrayed a new interest in contemporary composers.

Hahn was the son of a Catholic woman from Venezuela and a German-Jewish father; like Proust, he was half-Jewish, gay, and artistic. The family had emigrated from Venezuela to Paris in 1877 for political reasons. When he was five Reynaldo was already playing the piano; at age eight he was composing; and at ten he was studying at the Paris Conservatory. Between the ages of thirteen and eighteen he wrote his most celebrated songs, for which he is still known today to a small public.

When Marcel met him he had the velvety eyes and little mustache that Proust himself affected and so admired in other men (Flers and Daudet were two others who met these requirements). Very quickly Hahn and Proust became inseparable. The two young men traveled together and were put up in châteaus together by tolerant hostesses—extraordinary sophistication if one thinks that just across the Channel Oscar Wilde was being condemned to hard labor for practicing the same "vice." Robert de Montesquiou invited them as a couple to meet one of his titled relatives and the writer Maurice Barrès. Montesquiou took to referring to Hahn as Proust's "little brother," and Madame Lemaire received them in her château of Réveillon and begged them not to abandon her for a trip to Brittany, where they would be eating in hotels at irregular hours and ruining their health. (She would inspire Proust later when he would invent his character Madame Verdurin, similarly tyrannical in her attentions to her guests.) When they did leave, Hahn sent a letter to Madame Lemaire, saying, "How indulgent you have been toward us, we who are so crazy and so ill-mannered. What woman and what great artist would consent, as you have, to tolerate the caprices and the company of two old-fashioned young people?"

Hahn, in deference to Proust's admiration for the English aesthetic philosopher John Ruskin, would later compose, in 1902, *The Muses Lamenting the Death of Ruskin*, just as Proust would dedicate a new story, "The Death of Baldassare Silvande," to "Reynaldo Hahn, poet, singer, and musician." Perhaps a sign of the inevitable decline of their affair is that both works include in the title the word "death"—or perhaps that coincidence is merely due to the decadence of the period. Just a year after they met Hahn was already giving musical settings to Proust's portraits of painters and the two young men were planning to write a life of Chopin—a project that came to nothing. Very quickly Hahn was writing Proust letters in which the salutations varied in the space of three days from "My dear friend" to "Cher maître" to "My dear little one." From his end Proust was begging and bullying Hahn to rush to his side, and the tone is the same one Proust used when imploring his mother to give him another goodnight kiss.

Indeed, at this time Proust wrote another story, "The Confession of a Young Girl," in which the fourteen-year-old character says of her mother: "She came to my bedside to say goodnight, an old habit she had given up since I had taken too much pleasure in it as well as too much pain and had been unable to sleep because I kept calling her back to say goodnight one more time, something that towards the end I no longer dared to do, which made me feel all the more the need to do it and caused me to invent ever new pretexts such as the necessity to turn my hot pillow over or to chafe my freezing feet in her hands, which only she could do properly."

Something of this obsessive neediness shadowed Proust's love for Hahn, which led the younger man to write in his journal with paternal concern, "I would like so much to make him more stable. . . ." One of the most memorable scenes in *Swann's Way* occurs when Swann cannot find his mistress, Odette, and rushes in his coach from one closing café to another; at last he finally spots her and realizes that during this frantic search something has crystallized in him, a true passion for her, so different from the boredom and indifference he had felt just the day before. This famous scene had its antecedent in Proust's life when he was unable to find Reynaldo and nearly went mad. In the letter he wrote Hahn the next day he addressed him as "My poor child" and signed off as "Your child Marcel," a tribute both to his own infantilism and to his compassion for the beloved he could not resist tormenting with his affections.

He wrote:

> My little one, it's all Madame Lemaire's fault. She didn't want to let me go off to Madame E. Stern's without taking me there herself (along with Mademoiselle Suzette) so that at eleven o'clock when I wanted to leave she asked me to wait a few moments. I accepted especially because I kept hoping vaguely that you would arrive at the Daudets'. Had I been given the wrong time for the party when I was told eleven P.M. or had more time gone by than

I suspected? I felt it must be very late when I arrived at the Avenue Montaigne and saw people leaving the ball and no one entering. I couldn't not go in, since I didn't want to admit to Madame Lemaire that I had only one thought, which was to join you, my friend. Alas, I went into Madame Stern's, I spoke to no one, and I left, I can tell you, without having stayed more than four minutes and when I arrived at the Cambons' it was past 12:30! Flavie told me everything! Waiting for the little one, losing him, finding him again, loving him twice as much when I saw that he came back to Flavie's just to fetch me, expecting him during two minutes or making him wait for five minutes—there's the tragedy as far as I'm concerned, the throbbing, deep tragedy that someday I will write about perhaps and that in the meanwhile I am living through. . . .

The breathless style, the pell-mell grammar, the pressure of emotion all aptly re-create the experience, and the reference to Reynaldo in the third person ("the little one") reveals that Proust is already halfway towards creating a story out of the incident. Another sign of how tremulous their affair still was is that Proust constantly switches from the formal form for "you" (*vous*) to the informal (*tu*).

In 1895 the two young men traveled to Belle-Ile off the coast of Brittany to visit Sarah Bernhardt. On the Breton coast they stayed in a twenty-room hotel in the fisherman's village of Beg-Meil.

It was at Beg-Meil that Proust, who had already finished

if not yet published the stories constituting *Pleasures and Days*, began writing a novel, *Jean Santeuil*, a confused and not very successful book that prefigures *Remembrance of Things Past*, and which the young author would abandon before completing or in any way polishing. The two novels could not be more different in their tone and strategies. In *Jean Santeuil*, for instance, the stand-in for Proust is not a narrator but a character, referred to in the third person. Whereas in *Remembrance of Things Past* the parents are presented as wise, refined, melancholy beings who want nothing but their ailing, neurasthenic son's health and happiness (both parents were dead and sanctified by memory by the time Proust wrote *Remembrance*), in *Jean Santeuil* they are vulgar bullies and obstructionists who stand in the way of their son's social and artistic ambitions. Whereas the style of *Remembrance of Things Past* is olympian, philosophical, seamless, and all-encompassing, an ether in which all the characters revolve like well-regulated heavenly bodies, *Jean Santeuil* is written in jumps and starts, is full of quickly exhausted rages and enthusiasms, with several tries at the same scene, and in its hundreds of pages no theme develops and no incident produces a sequel. The characters make their cameo appearances but do not grow—or linger on in the imagination.

Since Proust had just emerged from years of school, classroom incidents play a large role in the text. Aristocrats already figure large in Proust's writing, but they are either grotesque caricatures or are unbelievably eager to entertain the timid, inconsequential Jean. Many of the characters whom Proust would later develop are already present in a germinating form. Similarly the Dreyfus Affair is already omnipresent, but it is studied more as political double-dealing than as an offstage event with lasting repercussions throughout the French social structure. Village life in Combray and military routine in a garrison town are already foreshadowed, as is the theme of involuntary memory. Male homosexuality, which would be a major subject in the later book, here is scarcely mentioned, although already Proust is disguising his boyfriends as girls, which leads to literary lesbianism. For example, in real life Hahn had known (and perhaps slept with) Lucien Daudet before Proust met either of them; this affair torments the jealous Jean, who suffers over thoughts of a "lesbian" dalliance between "Françoise" (Hahn) and "Charlotte" (Daudet). "Should I call this book a novel?" Proust asks. "It is something less, perhaps, and yet much more, the very essence of my life, with nothing extraneous added, as it developed through a long period of wretchedness. This book of mine has not been manufactured: it has been garnered." This idea, that life presents us with but one book to write, the story of our own existence which we must merely "translate," was one to which Proust would remain faithful.

In *Jean Santeuil* Hahn plays a role not only as the woman Françoise but also as the exquisite aristocrat Henri de Réveillon (named after Madame Lemaire's château); but in *Remembrance of Things Past* Hahn would be only faintly present. Already in *Jean Santeuil* Proust was ridding himself of Hahn by writing about him, since for Proust to paint the verbal portrait of a friend was to give him the kiss-off. If Proust never finished *Jean Santeuil*, it was partly because his love for Hahn was broken off before he got to the end of the book; and of course there were other, purely writerly reasons, such as his inability as yet to impose on his material any sort of form.

The affair with Hahn—one of the few equal and reciprocated and sustained sexual and romantic relationships of Proust's life—had begun in the spring of 1894 and had burned itself out two years later, although eventually the two became friends for life. At the height of their love Proust was able to declare, "I'd like to be master of all you might desire on earth so that I could bring it to you—author of everything that you admire in art so that I could dedicate it to you." Later, when they were just friends, it was to Hahn that Proust first read *Swann's Way*. Long after Proust's death, in 1945, Hahn became the director of the Paris Opéra. If the two young men shared a taste for music and literature, for travel and friendship, even for social climbing, at the same time their affair displayed the chief characteristics of love in a Proust story or novel: wild attacks of jealousy, recriminations and disputes, brooding and hurt feelings, and ecstatic reconciliations, all endured under the sign of love-as-war and courtship-as-strategy. Certainly Proust's most detailed and convincing portrait of love, that of Swann and Odette in *Swann's Way*, is based on the dynamics, the alternating bouts of jealousy and reconciliation, that characterized the youthful affair between Proust (Swann) and Hahn (Odette), even if there are few details derived from Hahn's life, looks, or personality.

The melancholy Hahn had already concluded: "The pleasure that love offers is not really worth the happiness that it destroys." In a similar vein Proust wrote, in "Critique of Hope in the Light of Love" (published in *Pleasures and Days*), that there is nothing worse than a collapse of trust in love, although if an end to trust kills love in the present and the future, it cannot affect *memories* of a shared past in a happier time: "Come closer, my dear little friend. Dry your eyes so that you can see—I don't know if tears are blurring my vision but I think I can pick out, over there, behind us, bonfires that are being lit. Oh! My dear little friend, how I love you. Give me your hand, let's go without getting too close to these fires. I think that it is Memory, indulgent and powerful, who wishes us well and is about to do so much for us, my dear."

Almost seamlessly Proust left Hahn for Lucien Daudet, who became his new focus of amorous interest in 1896 and 1897. Lucien was even younger than Reynaldo (and seven years younger than Proust), but wonderfully cultivated; he was nicknamed by his friends "Mister I-Know-Everything" (Monsieur Je-sais-tout), which also suggests he could be intolerably vain about his wisdom. Lucien's older brother

Léon declared that Lucien was the aristocrat of the family, and indeed Lucien (partly through his alliance with the empress Eugénie) rose far higher in society and for a longer time than Proust himself did. Although he was the son of one of the most celebrated writers of the day, Lucien was such a snob that he once remarked that he would have traded all his father's works for the chance to use the aristocratic *particule* and to call himself "d'Audet" instead of "Daudet." He was such a dandy that another member of the empress's court told him he was "overdressed" (using the English word) and that his ties were too pretty.

Marcel and Lucien shared a lively sense of humor as well as a taste for painting and literature. Lucien was adept at both arts, though he was crushed from the beginning by the example of his father as novelist and of their family friend Whistler as painter. As Lucien would write his mother in 1905 or 1906: "Whistler, whose only French student I was, instilled in me a certain taste in painting, led me to understand why something is beautiful, but at the same time he also gave me a great deal of scorn for whatever was not of the first rank and . . . this scorn I apply also to what I do." Later, of course, Lucien would feel totally eclipsed by Proust's monumental achievement, but also awed. The affair with Lucien, in any event, lasted no more than eighteen months, no longer than had the affair with Hahn. Proust and Lucien stayed friends, though Lucien frequently complained of neglect. Ever faithful in his fashion, however, Proust favorably reviewed Daudet's 1908 novel, the discreetly gay *Le Chemin mort*.

To please his parents Proust took a nonpaying job as a librarian, an "unremunerated attaché" at the Mazarine Library, housed in the same building as the French Academy. Typically, Proust pulled many strings to be named to this position, but as soon as he obtained it he worked with equal assiduity to take a medical leave, which was extended again and again until Proust was finally, years later, dismissed. As André Maurois, one of Proust's first biographers, put it: "He was the most detached of all attachés and went from leave to leave." Just as Flaubert had protected his time to write by working up medical reasons that kept him from practicing law (including a full-scale nervous breakdown), in the same way Proust, while pretending to humor his father's determination that he find a job, even an unremunerated one, managed in his passive-aggressive way to avoid doing anything he disliked for even so much as a day.

In 1896, when Proust was twenty-seven, his first book, *Pleasures and Days*, was finally published, although it had been ready for the printer for more than two years by that time. The holdup had been due to Madame Lemaire, who had taken her time sketching the floral designs that decorated the pages, and also to the difficulty of finding a publisher (at last Calmann-Lévy agreed, although he had many reservations about Proust's style). Even Anatole France, who wrote the preface, harbored his private misgivings;

according to his secretary, France complained that Proust wrote "sentences interminable enough to make you consumptive." In print, fortunately, France took another tone, although one still ambiguous. He said the stories breathed "an atmosphere of the hothouse among clever orchids" but also (continuing the vegetal metaphor) that they represented a renovation of classical learning: "This is the springtime of leaves on ancient branches."

When the book came out it appeared in such a luxurious edition that it cost four times the price of a normal volume its size. Sales were slow, especially since the reviews were few and tepid. Léon Blum, who in the future would preside over France, reviewed the book with considerable reservations (referring to "this book that is too coquettish and too pretty"). And even Proust's old school chum Fernand Gregh wrote an equivocal article: "The author of this book is commended to the public by the best known names; with a sort of timidity he has called on his most precious friends to introduce him into literary life. One could say that he has assembled around this newborn book all the good fairies. Usually one fairy is forgotten; but here all of them, it seems to us, have been convened. Each one has given to the child a grace: the first, melancholy; the second, irony; the third, a special music. And all have promised success." What Gregh was obviously satirizing in his silken way was Proust's penchant for publicity overkill, something that would reach its apogee years later when he invoked all the deities necessary to win the Goncourt Prize.

Between 1897 and 1899 Proust seems to have done little writing. *Pleasures and Days* (written between 1892 and 1895) had been published, and most of the work had been done on the never-completed *Jean Santeuil*, although Proust was still dramatizing and disguising in the novel his breakup with Hahn in the fictional affair between the characters Jean and Françoise, and he was adding details about the Dreyfus Affair even as they were occurring. In fact the nearly journalistic accounts of the Dreyfus trials contained in *Jean Santeuil* seriously compromised its proportions.

Of course in these years he was also reading constantly, primarily Balzac, the French writer who impressed him the most with his vast series of interlocking novels in which the characters keep reappearing. Proust was influenced by the story of how young, ambitious men from the provinces (epitomized by Lucien de Rubempré in *Lost Illusions*) could social-climb their way through Paris with the help of mistresses—and even a powerful male lover: Lucien, for instance, is aided by Vautrin, a master criminal who is clearly in love with him. Just as Balzac had learned the lore of the aristocracy from his titled friends and filled his books with detailed accounts of the Faubourg-Saint-Germain, in the same way Proust, helped by the aristocrats he was meeting through Robert de Montesquiou, was observing everything about this fabled bastion of the old aristocracy—and storing everything away in his memory for later use. To be sure, Proust himself made a distinction between normal memory—fallible, lifeless, virtually useless to the artist—and involuntary memory—perfect, vital, and timeless.

From Balzac Proust acquired a taste for the theatrical, evident in Proust's scenes in a male brothel, or in the moment when a lesbian spits on the photo of her friend's revered father, than dissolves into a frenzy of sexual excitement with her partner, or even in the great scene when the baron de Charlus (a literary cousin to both Balzac's Baron Hulot and Vautrin) is publicly rejected by a middle-class hostess but then grandly escorted out of the salon by the queen of Naples.

Proust was not influenced only by French authors. His reading tastes were international and included Shakespeare, Goethe, and George Eliot, though he read no language easily but French. He was especially frightened by George Eliot's portrait in *Middlemarch* of Casaubon, "who labored all his life on an insignificant and absurd work," as Proust put it (Proust was certainly haunted by the thought of this scholar who keeps promising to write and publish a Key to All Mythologies but finally sinks into confusion and sterility, unable to marshal his notes into coherence). In these years Proust also traveled to Holland to see a Rembrandt exhibition and wrote an article on the great Dutch painter. Even if his exasperated parents and relatives thought Marcel was nothing but a dilettante and a ne'er-do-well (he himself concurred most of the time), nevertheless he was slowly acquiring the cultural references and the life experiences—the knowledge of how society works and how love wounds—that he would need for his great book.

One of those experiences was challenging someone to a duel—and fighting it with pistols in the forest of Meudon, the traditional dueling ground southwest of Paris in the direction of Versailles. Jean Lorrain, a decadent novelist (and like Marcel a homosexual and inveterate partygoer), had a standing feud with Robert de Montesquiou. As a result he negatively reviewed Montesquiou's protégé's book *Pleasures and Days*, saying that Proust was "one of those pretty little society boys who've managed to get themselves pregnant with literature"; seven months later, on February 3, 1897, Lorrain returned to the attack with a newspaper article in which he wrote (under a pseudonym) that Alphonse Daudet was bound to write the preface of Marcel's next book, "since he cannot refuse anything to his son Lucien."

This suggestion that Proust was a homosexual having an affair with the young Daudet could not be allowed to pass by unchallenged. Three days later the two men, standing at a distance of twenty-five yards, fired in the air above each other's head: Proust reported that his bullet fell just next to Lorrain's foot. Proust showed a surprising coolness under fire. Perhaps he was proudest of the cachet of his seconds, the painter Jean Béraud and a celebrated he-man duelist, Gustave de Borda. No one remarked on the absurdity of one homosexual "accusing" another of being homosexual, which led to a duel to clear the "reputation" of the "injured" party. After the duel Lorrain left Proust alone, though he continued to attack Montesquiou (when the baron had his portrait painted by the society artist Boldini, Lorrain remarked in print that he had put himself in the hands of a painter of "little women," an artist known as "the Paganini of the Peignoir"). Proust challenged other men to duels over the years; none of them, fortunately, had tragic consequences. Although duels were considered anachronistic, most people still thought of a duelist as courageous and manly. It was this hypervirile image that Proust was eager to cultivate, as a way of offsetting his spreading reputation as a homosexual. To be *labeled* a homosexual in print (as opposed to living a homosexual life in private or discreetly among friends) was social anathema, even in Paris, until the very recent past.

VI

AFTER THE RELATIVE failure of *Pleasures and Days* and the eventual abandonment in 1899 of *Jean Santeuil* (which few of his friends even knew he was writing), Proust turned to translating the English aesthete and moralist John Ruskin. As Proust quickly discovered, there were two Ruskins—the art critic who was fascinated by French cathedrals and by Venice, and the social reformer, whose writings influenced Gandhi and the nascent Labour Party in England. Like other Victorians, including Dickens and Matthew Arnold, Ruskin was appalled by the effects of unbridled capitalism on the proletariat. Against the horrors of the machine age, Ruskin championed a utopian vision of the Middle Ages, the epoch of the independent artisan. Ruskin also called for an international movement of workers that would oppose war—an idea unlikely to appeal to Proust, who was a fierce patriot, a proud ex-soldier, and anything but a pacifist.

Between 1900 and 1906, Proust was entirely (if never uncritically) consumed by Ruskin and translated *The Bible of Amiens* and *Sesame and Lilies*. Since Marcel could not read English, he relied on a word-by-word trot provided by his mother and by a young Englishwoman named Marie Nordlinger, a cousin of Reynaldo Hahn. Proust adapted their literal translations into beautiful, idiomatic French. In order to prepare for his Ruskin work Proust traveled to Amiens with Hahn to look at the cathedral and to Venice with his mother. He also read mountains of books, including, in 1899, *The Religious Art of the Thirteenth Century in France* by Emile Mâle, and Robert de La Sizeranne's *Ruskin and the Religion of Beauty*, written in French, as well as those works of Ruskin that had already appeared in French translation. The style Proust worked out in French and retained for his later fiction, with its complex syntax and long sentences (so unusual in French literature), sounds very much like Ruskin.

It is difficult for people today to understand the enormous influence Ruskin (1819–1900) exerted everywhere in the last decades of the nineteenth century. In the United States aesthetes belonged to Ruskin Clubs; his doctrines, for instance, had a particular impact on the San Francisco Bay region shingle style of architecture with its adhesion to Arts and Crafts designs and techniques. But Ruskin's ideas were not just practical. They were primarily idealistic—an affirmation of the dignity of the individual in the face of urban anonymity, of the importance of culture in uplifting workingmen and -women. Even nature hikers invoked the name of Ruskin.

Proust responded to Ruskin's idealism, his anti-intellectualism, and his cult of beauty, but he was indifferent to his moral programs for the poor. Partly this indifference was attributable to the political distance between France, where reform was always staunchly anti-Catholic and secular and a matter of political struggle instead of sentimental compassion, and England, where most progressive schemes were tinged with Christian evangelism (Ruskin's mother had been extremely pious and had introduced him when he was still a child to the study of the Bible). But Proust had more personal objections to Ruskin. *Sesame and Lilies* is about the importance of reading as a way of improving the lot of the working class; whereas Proust prefaced his translation with one of his most moving texts, "On Reading," about the magical power of reading to awaken the imagination of a child—an end in itself.

Proust's essay on reading is his first mature piece of writing, the one in which he discovered the full, personal style that would characterize *Remembrance of Things Past*. Already he was writing about his childhood in the village that would become Combray. In his essay he contrasts his own aesthetic principles with those of Ruskin and associated figures in the Arts and Crafts movement such as William Morris:

> After lunch my reading began again immediately; especially if the day was a bit hot everyone went upstairs "to retire to their chambers," which permitted me to return right away by the little staircase with the small steps to my room on the only floor so low-ceilinged that a child

could have just jumped down from the overhanging windows and found himself in the street. I couldn't close my window without acknowledging the nod of the gunsmith across the street; pretending he had to lower his awnings, he stood in front of his door every day after lunch to smoke a cigarette and to say hello to the passersby who sometimes stopped to chat. The theories of William Morris, which have been so persistently applied by Maple and English decorators, decree that a bedroom is beautiful only to the degree that the things in it are useful and that every useful thing, even if it's only a simple nail, should not be concealed but rather exposed. On the bare walls of these hygienic bedrooms hang several reproductions of masterpieces above the bed and the brass rods with the curtains drawn back. If you judged it by the principles of this aesthetic, my bedroom was in no way attractive, for it was full of things that served no possible purpose and which modestly concealed those that did have a function— to the point of almost impeding their usefulness. But the beauty of my room, in my opinion, was due precisely to those things that weren't there for my convenience but had ended up there for the pleasure they offered. . . .

What is important to point out is that Proust's first genuine writing came in the form of a personal essay written in opposition to the theories of a major thinker. In a few years Proust's *Remembrance of Things Past* would grow out of a similar essay, conceived as a more violent argument against another aesthetic theorist. In this way, too, Proust was a forebear of his century. So much of the literary art of our times has struck sparks by opposing one genre to another—novel and memoir, for instance, or fiction and essay. We live in the epoch of the "nonfiction novel," of memoirs that take novelistic liberties with the truth, with biographies that stage discussions between the biographer and his long-dead subject (such as the fairly recent biography of Dickens by Peter Ackroyd, who "talks" to the nineteenth-century writer). Some critics have argued that creative energy is released when an inferior literary genre (the comic strip, for instance, or the mystery story) is elevated to the status of high art. One could just as easily contend that a similar heat is generated when two genres are rubbed against each other to form something entirely new. In Proust's case, the fertile encounter took place between the essay and the novel.

While Proust was working on his Ruskin translations and essays, he was becoming friendly with three young noblemen of a rank higher than that of any of his previous friends. The first he befriended was the count Gabriel de La Rochefoucauld, a liberal intellectual and a Dreyfusard—one of the models for Proust's character Robert de Saint-Loup, who has similarly advanced views. Just as Saint-Loup marries Gilberte Swann, who is half-Jewish, so Gabriel eventually married in 1905 Odile de Richelieu, a young heiress half-Jewish and half-ducal. The La Rochefoucaulds were one of the first three families of France, and accordingly Count Gabriel marked the pinnacle of French society—and of Proust's social climbing. Gabriel was famous for his frivolity, for his womanizing and sophisticated debauchery; one ancestor of his, a courtier at the time of Louis XIV, had been celebrated for his pithy, disillusioned epigrams, the *Maxims* of La Rochefoucauld, and now Count Gabriel was nicknamed "La Rochefoucauld of Maxim's"—especially appropriate since Maxim's in the Belle Epoque was known as a restaurant where no respectable woman would ever be seen.

Another handsome young aristocrat Proust became friendly with was the Romanian prince Antoine de Bibesco, who fended off Marcel's excessive demands on his time with a coolness that amounted to cruelty. Bibesco remembered that at one of his mother's salons he had first met Proust, whom he later characterized by saying he had eyes of "Japanese lacquer" and a hand that was "dangling and soft." When he subsequently instructed Marcel on how to shake hands with a virile grip, Proust said, "If I followed your example, people would take me for an invert." Which is just an indication of how devious the thinking of a homosexual of the period could become—a homosexual affects a limp handshake so that heterosexuals will not think he is a homosexual disguising himself as a hearty hetero—whereas in fact he is exactly what he appears to be: a homosexual with a limp handshake. . . .

Bibesco could be malicious, especially in the tricks he liked to play on his friends and the confidences he liked to betray. As Proust observed of him, he was serious about ideas but sarcastic with men. His nickname for Proust was "the Flatterer." When Proust confided in Bibesco his "nearly" amorous fascination with yet another young aristocrat, Bertrand de Fénelon, Bibesco instantly repeated the news on every side—which made Proust fear that he, Proust, would be accused of *salaïsme,* their private word for homosexuality, derived from the name of the notoriously gay Count Sala. Proust seems not to have realized how his reputation as a homosexual had become general knowledge in his circle. "We'd agreed," Proust wrote Bibesco, "that you would be the only one to whom I'd be open about what even Reynaldo isn't in on. Involuntarily you've informed the others about it. I've done everything to cover things up. But if now you're going to make allusions . . . ! Just think a moment about the effect that would have, about what people would think of me. . . . And not just me, there's also my family for whom I must not appear for any reason to be a salaïste, especially since I'm not one."

Despite such indiscretions, Bibesco paradoxically prided himself on his ability to keep a secret; in fact, being clandestine was a cornerstone of his friendships. He went so far as to propose to Marcel a pact in which the two friends would be obliged to repeat to each other all the good—and especially all the evil—they heard about each other through the rumor mill. This pact was accompanied by many code words—*tombeau* ("tomb"), for instance, meant that an inviolable secret was about to be pronounced. It may all sound rather juvenile, but Proust was thrilled at last to be part of a secret society of distinguished, handsome young heterosexuals, even if membership meant he must conceal his own sexual identity. Perhaps this fear of rejection, were the truth to be known, made Proust unduly dismissive of the prevailing French cult of friendship, for already in 1901 he was writing Bibesco, with whom it seems clear Proust was at least partially in love, "All that is to make too much of a fuss over friendship, a thing without reality. Renan says that we should flee intimate friendships. Emerson says that we must regularly trade in our friends for new ones. Of course people as great as they were have said the opposite. But I'm rather worn out by insincerity and by friendships, which almost come to the same thing." The "insincerity" Proust was complaining about was his own. Later, in the final volume of his great novel, Proust would write: "The artist who renounces one hour of work for an hour of chatting with a friend knows that he has sacrificed a reality for something that doesn't exist. . . ."

And yet while he was in the first flush of his friendship with Antoine de Bibesco he did everything to lure him to his sickbed—strangely enough, he even promised to discuss *salaïsme* with this incorrigible heterosexual: "I've reflected rather deeply about salaïsme and I'll communicate my thoughts to you during one of our next metaphysical interviews. Naturally enough my thoughts about it are extremely negative. But it does remain a philosophical point of curiosity about certain people. Dreyfusard, anti-Dreyfusard, salaïste, anti-salaïste are virtually the only interesting things to know about an idiot"—that is, we're always curious to know about the politics and sexuality of even an otherwise dull person.

Ironically, the handsome young Fénelon, the third of Proust's new friends, was also secretly homosexual, or rather bisexual (*bimettalisme* was the little group's code word for this tendency), a fact that Proust did not discover till years later. Proust was so infatuated with Fénelon that he called him "His Blue Eyes," after the name of a popular play of the day. During a trip to Holland the two men had a temporary falling out. As Proust wrote Hahn, "My affection for his blue eyes is undergoing an unhappy crisis just now, since when he said something unpleasant to me I started socking him with both fists." It was Fénelon who once gallantly aided a shivering Proust by walking agilely over the backs of the booths in a crowded restaurant to fetch his coat—exactly as Saint-Loup would later do in *Remembrance of Things Past*. Indeed, Proust created his characters by combining the traits of several different friends. But he could also split one real friend through mitosis into several different characters. Thus when Marcel developed a crush on Fénelon he enlisted Bibesco to spy on him and to report on his movements—exactly as the Narrator would do in his fits of jealousy over Albertine. Spying, secret investigations, long hours of interrogation—such was Proust's form of love: juridical passion, or love-as-trial.

With his new friends Proust shared a taste for medieval

architecture; Proust's enthusiasm was inspired by Ruskin, no doubt. Proust and Antoine de Bibesco and Antoine's brother Emmanuel, along with other friends, liked to make excursions to the Gothic churches in the Paris region and even beyond. The first trip was to the magnificent cathedral of Chartres. Then in the spring of 1902 Proust went in two motorcars with the two Bibesco brothers, Fénelon, and other friends to Provins (beyond the current site of Disneyland Paris); and on a slightly later trip with the same group, as far away as Laon, eighty-seven miles from Paris. There Proust was impressed by the belfries of the cathedral, decorated by the sculpted heads of eight colossal oxen; the oxen and many other details he observed in this church and others would work their way into his meticulous descriptions in *Remembrance of Things Past*. Today most writers of fiction avoid comparing their characters to already existing works of art, but Proust was never afraid of creating a highly aestheticized atmosphere. In fact he intensifies the aestheticism to such a point that it becomes an incontrovertible element of his style. The Guermantes family gets compared to those stone oxen and the creatures in Noah's ark. The painter Elstir discusses scenes from the life of the Virgin which Marcel had also observed at the church in Laon, and women he admires are compared to women in Renaissance Italian paintings.

Later in 1902 Proust traveled to Bruges in Belgium to see an exhibition of Flemish masters. With Fénelon he traveled to Holland, where for the first time he saw Vermeer's

The View of Delft—the very painting that he, Proust, would study again in Paris shortly before his death and that his character Bergotte (the novelist based on Anatole France) would see before collapsing in the museum.

At the end of 1902 Fénelon was appointed as a diplomat to Constantinople and Proust admitted he was living through "truly despairing hours."

VII

WHEN PROUST BEGAN his translations of Ruskin and his essays on him, the closed, stable world of his family and domestic routine was still intact, but by the time he had concluded them everything had changed catastrophically. On February 2, 1903, his brother, Robert, married Marthe Dubois-Amiot. Later the same year, on November 26, Proust's father died, a day after the birth of Robert Proust's daughter Suzy. Two years later, on September 26, 1905, his beloved mother would die of nephritis after a long, painful illness. She was just fifty-six. As Proust wrote at the time, "My life has now lost its only goal, its only sweetness, its only love, its only consolation." Later he would add, "In dying, Maman took with her her little Marcel." The sentence can be interpreted, if the emphasis is placed on "little," to mean that the ineffectual, dandified, immature Marcel died at her death, to be reborn as the determined, wise, ascetic Proust.

For the rest of his life he would mourn her with extra intensity on the anniversary of her death—even on monthly anniversaries of the fatal day. And yet Proust was also capable of later writing, "In this world of ours where everything withers, everything perishes, there is a thing that decays, that crumbles into dust even more completely, leaving behind still fewer traces of itself, than beauty: namely grief." Despite this clearsightedness, Proust became a master of the consoling (or at least wonderfully understanding) condolence letter—always pouring into each one something of that dark, crippling grief he had felt at the death of his parents.

Just before she died, Madame Proust had reluctantly allowed herself to be photographed; in *Remembrance of Things Past* the Narrator's grandmother makes a similar gesture, in order to leave behind a last image of herself for a grieving grandson. Indeed, in his vast novel Proust assigns to the character of the mother the feelings his real mother had had of disappointment with her son's lack of self-discipline; whereas to the figure of the fictional grandmother he lends his real mother's tenderness, her unconditional love for him in spite of all his failings. As Proust himself viewed the matter, "the lack of will power which prevents a man from resisting any vice in particular" is "that greatest of all vices." He would often look at the photo of his mother; indeed, he studied his collection of photos all the time whenever he wrote.

Perhaps the strangest drama in Proust's life is the transformation of little Marcel—the dandy and partygoer, the time waster who at age thirty-four had managed to do little more than write a slim volume of short stories and two translations of Ruskin—into the great Proust, who wrote one of the longest and most remarkable novels of all time. One psychological clue to Proust's endless stalling before beginning his novel is provided near the end of that very book: "No doubt, my idleness having given me the habit, when it was a question of work, of putting it off from one day to another, I imagined that death too might be postponed in the same fashion." Like the man who superstitiously refuses to write a will out of an unacknowledged fear that by doing so he will be signing his death warrant, in the same way Proust fancied that so long as he failed to begin his life's work, his life would go on.

The artistic reason for his long delay was that his ambition was so great—a desire to write a book that would rival Balzac's panorama of Parisian society, and to combine that scope with an intimate history of a young man's artistic and spiritual evolution. This ambition required so many technical skills as a writer—everything from a traditional, Dickensian knack at rendering eccentrics to a psychological penetration worthy of the great Russians—that Proust could never have begun to forge them into a flowing, viable style before his late thirties. Meanwhile, the circumstances of his life were conspiring to prepare him, for if his innate sociability gave him the knowledge of the world he needed for the panoramic aspects of his book, his endless hours of suffering as a solitary invalid provided him with the depth and introspection he needed for the masterful pages that anatomize the passions. Proust was one of the few twentieth-century writers who possessed both a grasp of how society works and a sufficient distance from it to view it objectively and then to write about it. Moreover, he had the necessary drive to write an unprecedentedly long and comprehensive book, since only by doing so could he prove that his endless dithering and fruitless preparations had paid off.

He also had a large enough fortune to buy the freedom necessary to undertake such a vast and uncertain project. While his parents were still alive he had been kept on a very tight financial leash. They begrudged him the lavish expenses of every dinner he gave and provided him with such a small allowance that he was unable to move out of the family apartment. In his letters to his mother from a health resort he would calculate the cost of every meal, every bouquet offered to a lady, every cab ride, and part of the solitude of these years was due not so much to ill health as to straitened circumstances; as a young man he'd made the occasional splashy gesture (inviting Madame Straus and her son to the opera, for instance) but had sacrificed to it all the small, normal outings that nourish most friendships.

Three and a half months after his mother's death Proust discovered that he had inherited the equivalent of about $6 million of our money today, including a monthly revenue of some $15,000; his brother received the same amount. Both Marcel and Robert were astonished, since their parents had always pled poverty and practiced the strictest economies. Now that Proust was more than comfortably settled, he still persisted in feeling that he was always on the verge of bankruptcy, an utterly unfounded fate he was always tempting by buying friends extravagant gifts—bejeweled watches, paintings, diamond-studded cigarette cases, Gallé vases, even the airplane which he ordered for his beloved chauffeur Agostinelli but which he was able to cancel after the chauffeur's sudden death. (In his novel the Narrator offers to buy Albertine a yacht.) Proust gave good advice to friends on love, money, and health, but when making decisions affecting himself in these same domains, he solicited absolutely everyone's advice, then, disastrously, followed none of it. He made many ruinous investments but refused to listen to his banker. He bought when a stock was high and sold when it was low. More often than not he purchased a stock because of its poetic name ("The Tanganyika Railway," "The Australian Gold Mines"); in fact, these stocks were a substitute for the travels to exotic places he longed to make. He wore shabby clothes and invited large parties to the Ritz. He regularly tipped 200 percent. According to one famous anecdote he borrowed a large sum from the doorman at the Ritz and then promptly gave him back the money as a tip. Yet he took no interest in collecting paintings or books or even in buying clothes or refurbishing his apartment. He was a playboy-monk.

He felt that his parents' apartment was too large for him and far too expensive—and too full of memories. As he wrote one friend, "I went into certain rooms of the apart-ment where for one reason or another I hadn't been in a while and I explored unknown parts of my suffering which stretched out infinitely the farther I proceeded. There is a certain floorboard near Maman's room that always creaks when you tread on it and as soon as Maman would hear it she'd purse her lips with that little noise that means: come kiss me."

On December 26, 1906, he moved to an apartment at 102 boulevard Haussmann that had belonged to his great-uncle Louis Weil (the now-deceased old man who had been Laure Hayman's protector). Upon his uncle's death Proust had inherited a quarter of the building, but unfortunately he let his aunt buy out his share, which meant that he ended up a mere renter without any rights—a situation that would eventually turn drastically against him. It was another of his impractical decisions, though in his defense it should be pointed out that Proust at this time was looking for a house in the country ("but not in the trees," he insisted, ever alert to causes of asthma attacks) and was determined to leave Paris.

The apartment was in itself ill-suited to an asthmatic writer sensitive to noise since it was located near the huge department store Printemps, not far from the Saint-Lazare train station, and was on one of the principal arteries of the new Paris—a boulevard full of dust and clamor, lined with chestnut trees heavy with the pollen that sent Proust into sti-fling crises. Yet Proust was attracted to the six-room apartment because he had often come to dine there with his mother, and he could not accept to live somewhere that his mother had never known. Perhaps he liked it, too, because it looked out on the melancholy Chapel of Atonement to Louis XVI, which had been built after the Restoration to expiate the sins of the nation for guillotining its ruler.

To insulate his bedroom, where he wrote, he lined the walls with cork in 1910—an idea he got from the poet Anna de Noailles, who had picked up the tip from the successful playwright Henry Bernstein, another martyr to noise. There he inhaled his fumigations of medicinal Legras powder, which floated out into the hallway and caused the neighbors to protest against the smell. The windows were hung with layers of heavy curtains that were never opened. Light, noise, and above all dust were excluded as thoroughly as possible. When Proust would go to Cabourg for his annual summer holiday the whole apartment would be vacuumed with a special machine by workmen, who cleaned every book, every picture frame, every slipcover, and every cornice. Today his apartment has been restored by the SNVB bank that occupies the building and is open to tourists once a week. It was never, however, much to look at, since Proust feared dust-breeding furniture and wanted his apartment to resemble a hospital. The furniture he did have consisted of the heavy, dark pieces saved from his parents' apartment.

It was in this unpromising new apartment, however, that Proust wrote most of *Remembrance of Things Past*. The mammoth book began, appropriately enough, as a sort of Platonic dialogue with his mother on the subject of Sainte-Beuve, the nineteenth-century literary critic, whose ideas and writing galled Proust. He had begun to think about Charles-Augustin Sainte-Beuve with renewed intensity at the end of 1904 and the beginning of 1905, when everyone was celebrating the centennial of the critic's birth (December 23, 1804). In gushing terms contemporary eulogists assured their readers that Sainte-Beuve's reputation was now unassailable—a claim that doubly irritated a dissenting Proust.

Sainte-Beuve was the founder of the "biographical" method; he believed that one could not even begin to read Balzac, for instance, much less evaluate his work, if one did not first know everything available about his life, based on his letters, journals, and the accounts of his friends and acquaintances. Sainte-Beuve wanted to know an author's religious views, his response to nature, his behavior with women, with money, with the rich and the poor. "What was his routine, the style of his daily life?" Sainte-Beuve asked. "What were his vices; his weaknesses? None of the answers to these questions is irrelevant in judging the author of a book and the book itself. . . ." What Proust objected to right away was the fact that by using this method Sainte-Beuve had seriously underestimated, even dismissed, three of the greatest writers of his era: Stendhal, Baudelaire, and Nerval.

Because Sainte-Beuve had known Stendhal personally, he assured his readers that Henri Beyle (to use Stendhal's real name) would have been the first to be astonished by his present fame. This urbane nonsense, based on Sainte-Beuve's earnest misreading of Beyle's modesty, made Proust chortle cruelly. For Proust the most important sign of a critic's skill was his or her evaluation of contemporaries, given that everyone agreed about the relative importance of the writers of the past. Secondly, Proust believed that housed within the same artist was a social being—someone who went to parties, paid calls on ladies, hobnobbed with critics—and a creative being, the one who invented music, poetry, painting, or prose. And Proust was convinced that there was very little relationship between these two separate beings: "A book is the product of a different self from the one we manifest in our habits, our social life and our vices." But if Proust thought the life could not explain the work, he was nonetheless fascinated by the biographies of artists. He didn't object to biography as a form; he was only against biographical criticism.

With his usual procrastination, Proust, while lying in his sickbed and inhaling his fumigations, thought out the various aspects of his attack on Sainte-Beuve, but as yet committed nothing to paper. As he wrote Lucien Daudet, "When I read myself and especially when I write—(for I never read myself)—(it's also true that I never write anymore either) . . . I find that I have no talent, that I haven't known how, for many different reasons, to turn my gifts into talent, and my style has gone rotten without ever ripening."

In fact, he was far too ill to work. Sometimes he would have as many as ten asthma attacks a day, and usually he was too weak even to walk from one room to another. As late as December 1908 he wrote his friend Georges de Lauris, "I'm going to write something on Sainte-Beuve. I have more or less two articles in mind (magazine articles): one is an essay of the standard sort [and] the other would begin with the story of a morning: Maman would come near my bed and I would tell her about the article that I want to do on Sainte-Beuve, and I would develop the idea for her." He added that his mind was as heavy as a full trunk with all the things he wanted to say. But three months later he still had not jotted down a single line of either essay.

In a letter of this period he said he was planning: a study of the nobility; a Parisian novel; an essay on Sainte-Beuve and Flaubert; an essay on women; and an essay on pederasty. Other topics mentioned were gravestones, stained-glass church windows—and an essay on the novel. What is crucial to underline is that at its very inception Proust thought of his book as *several* books, mostly essays. Only gradually did he see that he could bind all these diverse subjects together into a single work and that he could call it neither a memoir, nor an essay, nor a pastiche, but rather a novel. Proust had always been drawn to writers who had confused genres: he was thinking admiringly, for instance, of Baudelaire's prose poems, or of the autobiographical side of Flaubert's novel *A Sentimental Education*. But where Proust differed from all his predecessors was in the gigantism of his project, a first-person narrative that would be not only the most penetrating analysis of several psyches but also a vast panorama of society—a book, in short, that would be as deep as it was wide.

VIII

———

BY JUNE 1908, Proust was in the full flood of composition. By July he wrote another friend, his school chum Robert Dreyfus, "It's been sixty hours since—I won't say slept, but since I've turned off the electric lights." He had obviously rejected the traditional essay on Sainte-Beuve he had proposed and was working instead on the fictional version of a morning devoted to discussing Sainte-Beuve with his mother. Even when he went to Cabourg at the end of August he spent most of his day shut up in his hotel room writing. At the same time he was already stewing about the problem of publishing such a manuscript, which he judged "obscene." Obviously the novel had gone far beyond a polite literary discussion with his mother. As he told Georges de Lauris in a letter labeled "Confidential and rather urgent": "I am finishing a novel that despite its provisional title, *Against Sainte-Beuve, Memories of a Morning*, is a real novel, and a novel extremely immodest in certain parts. One of the main characters is a homosexual. The name of Sainte-Beuve is not introduced casually. The book ends with a long conversation on Sainte-Beuve and aesthetics."

In fact, *Remembrance of Things Past* does indeed end with a long meditation (not conversation) on aesthetics, but Sainte-Beuve had long since been absorbed into the very texture of Proust's narrative: the *character* Vinteuil is a mighty creator as a composer and a totally self-effacing wimp as a *man*—the perfect counterargument to Sainte-Beuve's theory of the harmonious congruity between an individual's life and work. What is equally interesting is that homosexuality (including lesbianism), to which Proust would devote nearly a quarter of *Remembrance of Things Past*, was part of his conception from the very beginning, and that from the beginning he recognized this subject might make the whole book unpublishable.

Although he was only thirty-eight, Proust feared he might soon be dead. He was so ill that he was spending about twenty thousand dollars a year for medicines. He wrote: "One no longer considers oneself to be more than the trustee, who can vanish at any moment, of intellectual secrets, which will vanish too, and one would like to check the inertia that proceeds from one's previous lethargy by obeying Christ's beautiful commandment in St. John: 'Work while ye have the light.'" Everything he would write over the next fourteen years would be indited under the sign of imminent mortality.

But Proust had not yet withdrawn from society to devote himself entirely to work. In 1908 he was still seeing many people, partly as a way of acquiring documentation for his writing. At Cabourg, for instance, he studied the actress Lucy Gérard and the two daughters of Viscount d'Alton, models for the young girls described in *Within a Budding Grove*, although he had a still more acute eye trained on a little bevy of handsome youths, to whom he sent tender letters.

According to Henri Bonnet's *Marcel Proust de 1907 à 1914*, it was this band of boys, met casually on the beach and observed with feverish fascination, who directly inspired Proust's novelistic description of the undifferentiated group of girls in bloom. The transpositions Proust made are obvious in his journals. For instance, in *Within a Budding Grove* a young woman, Andrée, impresses the Narrator initially when she leaps over an old man on the beach, although later he loses interest in her after she explains that she is in reality as neurasthenic as the Narrator and has become athletic only under doctor's orders. But in his notebooks Proust writes, "I linked myself with an eminent sportsman who seemed my polar opposite and whose company would provide a calming cure for my exhausted nerves—and he told me that if he played so many sports it was only to cure his neurasthenia."

His special favorite was nineteen-year-old Marcel Plantevignes, who visited Proust in his room nearly every day for hours, listening to Proust's novel-in-progress, until one afternoon a mocking young lady warned Plantevignes against Proust's "special morals." When Proust learned that

Plantevignes had made no protest against the accusation, he went into a rage against the boy and even challenged Plantevignes's father to a duel, by now a familiar reflex when Proust imagined his honor had been compromised. Since Proust was entirely silent about the nature of the offense, Plantevignes could not begin to imagine what he had done wrong. Even Proust's "seconds" (one of whom was the viscount d'Alton) could not stop laughing at the absurdity of the challenge, especially since Proust had intimated he would fire in the air above Monsieur Plantevignes's head. They kept calling it a "duel from an operetta by Offenbach."

At last Proust dropped a hint about what had so offended him. As Plantevignes, at last enlightened, later recalled:

> Suddenly I saw that brief scene again. The encounter on the promenade had been so quick and fortuitous that I had never thought about it. She was a young woman very fond of teasing, who often teased Proust about homosexuality and who, when she had met me on the promenade, had stopped me again to warn me and cast her terrible aspersions. "I know, I know, Madame, what you're going to tell me," I had answered quickly, "but it has no importance as far as I'm concerned. Excuse me, Madame, goodbye, I'm in a big hurry." And I had fled as quickly as possible.

The young lady had told Proust soon afterwards that Plantevignes had agreed with her by replying to her charges, "Yes, I know all about it, but it's all the same to me." When Proust confronted the boy directly, asking him, "How did you know what she was going to say?" the exasperated Plantevignes replied, "Because that's what everyone's whispering on the promenade." A stunned, pale Proust absorbed the news, then finally stated sarcastically, "How charming to arrive somewhere preceded by one's reputation."

When Plantevignes assured Proust that he did not believe the gossip, nor did his parents, the writer was at last mollified, although he warned Plantevignes not to talk about their friendship to strangers. Then both men exchanged a mocking, merry glance. "And our mutual enthusiasm," Plantevignes recalled, "suddenly released from all constraint, became so boyish and comical that we burst out laughing simultaneously, drowning our recent estrangement in a resolution sumptuous with joy."

Soon Proust was again tranquilly admiring this young man, a spirit "still in flower," as he put it in a letter written at the time—a reference that is a flash-forward to the French title for what is called in English *Within a Budding Grove*. The original, French title is translated as the more elaborate *In the Shadow of Young Girls in Flower—A l'ombre des jeunes filles en fleur*—a title, moreover, that Plantevignes claims he suggested to Proust, even though he offered it with all due apologies for its "period" sound and its operetta lightness.

By mid-August 1909 Proust was proposing to an editor a

book he'd nearly finished and which he called a novel—and which he described in a way that resembles some aspects of *Remembrance of Things Past*, though it was far shorter and contained only a few of the incidents and themes developed at such length in the finished book. At this time he was talking of a novel of about 300 pages (instead of the eventual 4,300), which he said would be followed by a 150-page conversation about Sainte-Beuve.

Fortunately the editor refused the novel-essay that Proust proposed in 1909. Then, after a second editor failed to serialize the book in a newspaper, Proust became less frantic and worked quietly on his novel for the next three years. When he had first conceived his novel, the entire "Swann in Love" section which makes up four-fifths of the first volume of *Remembrance of Things Past* had not yet been thought up. Originally the story had proceeded directly from "Combray," the story of the Narrator's childhood summers in a village with his father's relatives, to a description of his play with Gilberte Swann in the gardens of the Champs-Elysées and his adolescent love for her. But when the volume *Swann's Way* was finally published in November 1913, most of it was devoted to a story that took place before the Narrator's birth and during his childhood. Charles Swann, who like Proust is Jewish and an aesthete brilliantly connected socially, takes up with a kept woman, Odette. At first Swann is almost indifferent to Odette, but gradually he comes to prize her—in his best aesthetic style—because he recognizes her resemblance to a figure in a Botticelli painting, and because he associates her with the hypnotic "little phrase" he hears in a sonata by the (fictional) composer Vinteuil. His passion, however, is ignited only one night when he fails to find her (in the scene that recalls Proust's own frantic search for Reynaldo Hahn).

The love affair between Swann and Odette is played out against a social backdrop, the salon of Madame Verdurin, a rich middle-class woman who pretends she is so sensitive that the sound of beautiful music makes her physically ill, and who brands all those aristocrats who she knows would never accept her invitations as "bores." In many ways Madame Verdurin resembles the equally tyrannical and artistic Madame Lemaire, who years before had taken such a benign attitude towards Proust's affair with Hahn.

The "Swann in Love" section introduces the idea that love is never reciprocated, a theme that later in the book is replayed in the Narrator's tormented affair with Albertine. It contrasts comic scenes about society with moments of intensely private introspection, which will characterize the entire seven volumes. It plays Swann, a failed writer, against the Narrator, who, though his vocation is long delayed, eventually becomes a fulfilled writer—the very genius who has written the masterpiece we are now reading. And it suggests that one reason for Swann's failure is his addiction to friendship and frivolity and especially to "idolatry," by which Proust meant the collector's love of fine furnishings, beautiful mistresses, and great paintings: the perishable Things of this world rather than the immortal ideas that lie behind them, which can be recaptured only through involuntary memory—and which only then can be codified in great works of literary art.

What Proust had discovered since writing *Jean Santeuil* was how to take up themes, let them drop, then come back to them, though each time the theme was exposed to a different light. No longer did Proust feel that he had to say everything at once or to set in stone his opinions on every character and topic. Now the dramatic twists of the plot dictated the insights revealed to the Narrator. He'd also learned how to introduce a character through hearsay—the (false) rumors, for example, that Charlus is a hypervirile womanizer who despises homosexuals and is Odette's lover, misinformation that the reader picks up long before being introduced to Charlus himself. During the course of the seven volumes of *Remembrance of Things Past* the Narrator is puzzled by Charlus's extreme friendliness that alternates with bouts of insufferable—and inexplicable— rudeness. Then, halfway through *Remembrance of Things Past*, the Narrator observes Charlus cruising a tailor, Jupien, who is entirely receptive to his advances. This insight into Charlus's sexuality also explains his unnatural attachment to a cruel and ungrateful, if talented, violinist, Morel. Charlus's masochism becomes even clearer during the air raids of World War I, when the Narrator seeks shelter in a building that turns out to be a male brothel owned by the same Jupien. There the Narrator observes Charlus being chained and beaten by hired hustlers. This sexual humiliation alternates with his moments of over-weening pride and arrogance in society—until, at the end of the whole cycle, a feeble, snowy-haired Charlus, accompanied by an ever faithful Jupien, salutes and bows to every passerby, afraid he might be snubbing someone important whose identity he can no longer recall.

As the trajectory of this single character demonstrates, Proust had learned a method of presentation that falls midway between that of Dickens and that of Henry James. Dickens assigns his characters one or two memorable traits, sometimes highly comic, which they display each time they make an appearance; James, by contrast, is so quick to add nuances to every portrait that he ends up effacing them with excessive shading. Proust invented a way of showing a character such as Charlus in Dickensian bold relief at any given moment—Charlus as the enraged queen or, later, Charlus as the shattered King Lear. Yet, by building up a slow composite of images through time, Proust achieves the same complexity that James had aimed at, though far more memorably. It's like the old dispute among painters as to the primacy of line or of shading. Dickens could draw with a firm bounding line but used so little shading he gave no sense of perspective. James was all shading and depth, but (especially in his late novels) nothing vigorous distinguished the profile of one character from another. Proust succeeded in rendering characters with the same startling simplicity as Dickens but generated a lifelike subtlety and motion by giving us successive "takes" over hundreds of pages. In that way his style is like the magic lantern the Narrator watches at bedtime when he's a boy. The heat of the lamp causes a band of images to turn and to project the illusion of motion on the wall. In the same way Proust's slide show of portraits of the same character induces the illusion of duration, of development—and of psychological truth.

Proust had a lively eye for self-satire and could delegate his own peevishness to Charlus, his jealous rages to Swann, his snobbishness to the duchesse de Guermantes—and not merely the general outlines of these feelings but even highly specific incidents portrayed in his novel.

In the years 1909–11 Proust rewrote and expanded the first volume of his novel. He now came up with a way of constantly adding details and observations to his manuscript. Indeed, his way of rewriting was to add. First he would expand as he dictated to his stenographers. Then he would have his manuscript set in type (Proust used typesetters the way other people use typists, or word processors). Finally he would begin to crowd the margins with more and more new passages, all designed to enrich his design and to establish links among the various characters and scenes. These additions would sometimes become so copious that Proust would have to paste in new pages. The cost of resetting the type would run very high—which Proust gladly paid. In fact, if any writer would have benefited from a word processor it would have been Proust, whose entire method consisted of adding details here and there and of working on all parts of his book at once, like one of those painters who like to keep a whole canvas "in motion" rather than patiently perfecting it section by section, one after another.

In 1910 Proust toiled on what would become *Swann's Way* and *The Guermantes Way*. The next year he organized his book into two volumes, one of which would be entitled *Time Lost* and the other *Time Regained*. As he became more and more obsessed with his novel, he wrote fewer articles and hardly went out at all. His fascination with all the arts, however, would occasionally tempt him to attend a concert, see a ballet or opera, or visit a gallery; in these years he was especially intrigued by the Ballets Russes, directed by the greatest impresario of the day, Sergei Diaghilev, and starring the dancer Nijinsky, Diaghilev's lover. On the opening night of *The Rite of Spring*, Proust saw the revolutionary ballet and afterwards, according to a letter he wrote at the time, dined with Diaghilev and Nijinsky as well as with the composer, Stravinsky, and Proust's new friend the very young and brilliant writer Jean Cocteau. When Diaghilev commissioned Reynaldo Hahn to write a score for a ballet, *Le Dieu bleu,* Proust wept with pride.

In 1911 Proust became a subscriber to Théâtrophone, a service that held a telephone receiver up at a concert, which allowed people to stay at home and hear live music on their receivers. Thanks to this novel system, Proust was able to listen to Wagner (on February 20, 1911, for instance, he heard Act III of *Die Meistersinger*) and to Debussy's opera *Pelléas et Mélisande* (with Maggie Teyte as Mélisande).

As the years of composition of his great epic went by, years when Proust was discouraged and afraid that he would never finish it, he would compare it to a Gothic church always expanding but left incomplete, or to the long and ambitious four-opera *Ring* cycle by Wagner. Proust preferred Wagner to Debussy, the fully developed score to the hints and sketches of *Pelléas et Mélisande*.

Proust esteemed Wagner's way of "spitting out everything he knew about a subject, everything close or distant, easy or difficult." This sort of fullness and explicitness he obviously preferred in literature as well, an amplitude he contrasted favorably to the pared-back reticence of the neoclassical style, as it was practiced by Anatole France or even André Gide. Still more important, Wagner's opera *Parsifal* has been designated by some critics as the very template for *Remembrance of Things Past*, since both works trace the quest of a young man—in *Parsifal*, for the Holy Grail; and in Proust's book, for the secret of literature. Proust's "young girls in flower" may be compared to the Flower Maidens in *Parsifal*, the Guermantes clan (with distant origins in Germany) to Wagner's Guernemanz, head of the Holy Grail Knights, and so on.

By 1912 Proust had written some 1,200 pages and was ready to submit the *Swann's Way* that we know to various editors. This first part, some 712 pages in length, had been typed by a young man named Albert Nahmias, an intelligent secretary who did not hesitate to make marginal comments about the scenes he was transcribing from Proust's endless notebooks. Proust was so fond of the handsome Nahmias that he wrote him: "If I could only change my sex, face and age and take on the looks of a young and pretty woman so that I could kiss you with all my heart." Albert Nahmias contributed his name to the character Albertine, though when someone asked him if he had been the model for that character, he responded modestly, "There were several of us." Proust himself wrote that there had been many models for Albertine, including some he had forgotten, since "a book is a great cemetery in which one can no longer read the names on most of the tombs." In fact the numerous originals for Albertine may explain why the character is so vague, despite the fact that more pages are devoted to her than to any other character except the Narrator (her name is mentioned 2,360 times). Even the exact location of her beauty mark keeps migrating from her chin to her lip to below her eye. As Julia Kristeva, who has written a trenchant critical book about Proust and time, remarks, these young women in Cabourg are never perceived in Proust as individuals but more as a "group" or a "swarm." Typically, an event performed by Andrée in one passage is assigned to Gisèle five hundred pages later.

Proust was becoming so immersed in his writing that soon his life was imitating his work. When Albert Nahmias stood Proust up one evening in 1912 at Cabourg (Proust did not know the reason—a car accident), Proust wrote him a letter that directly echoed Swann's declarations to Odette:

"I have a lively affection for you that sometimes makes me want to yawn, sometimes to weep, sometimes to drown myself." Before long, however, the friendship was patched up and Nahmias and a young English secretary were working again on the typescript, first in Cabourg, then in Paris.

On October 28, 1912, Proust's novel was submitted through powerful intermediaries to the Parisian publisher Fasquelle—a strange choice, since it was the house that had published the naturalists Flaubert, Zola, and the Goncourt brothers. Proust justified the choice of such a big, commercial publisher by saying rather airily that he hoped thereby to reach "people who take trains and before boarding them buy a badly printed volume." On December 24 the manuscript was returned, the reader's report declaring, "After 712 pages of this manuscript . . . one has no notion, no notion at all of what it's all about. . . . What does all this mean? Where is it all leading? Impossible to know anything about it! Impossible to say anything about it!"

Even before Fasquelle had turned him down, Proust was already making overtures to a new publishing house which put out the distinguished literary magazine *La Nouvelle Revue Française* and which would eventually come to be known as Gallimard. The house had been started by André Gide, Jacques Copeau, and Jean Schlumberger, three brilliant literary lights, with its business affairs handled by Gaston Gallimard. Proust had been a subscriber to the magazine since 1911 and admired many of its writers, such as Valéry Larbaud (James Joyce's first French translator and a sophisticated, accomplished prose stylist in his own right) and Paul Claudel (the arch-Catholic playwright and diplomat). Proust even went so far as to offer to underwrite the expenses of publishing his book. He explained to the sensitive, patrician Gallimard that in the second volume—which at the time Proust thought would be the last—a pederast would be introduced: "I think the character is rather an original one," Proust said, "he's the virile pederast, in love with virility, loathing effeminate young men, in fact loathing all young men, just as a man who has suffered through women becomes a misogynist." Although Proust hastened to assure Gallimard that "a metaphysical and moral viewpoint is maintained throughout . . . nevertheless, the old gentleman seduces a male concierge and keeps a pianist." To be sure, the pianist became a violinist and the concierge a tailor, but otherwise Proust was being perfectly accurate about a character who would eventually be called Charlus, but who at the time was still identified as Monsieur de Fleurus or de Guray.

Once again Proust met with disappointment. The committee of readers, led by Gide, seems not even to have read the manuscript, much less to have prepared a report. They were put off by Proust's reputation as a socialite and snob, a friend of duchesses, as well as by his endless, flowery sentences. If we compare Proust's style with Gide's we can immediately see what the committee objected to. In Gide's

The Immoralist, a 130-page novel finished in 1901, the writing is very pared back: "Toward the end of January, the weather suddenly changed for the worse; a cold wind began blowing, and my health immediately showed the effects. . . . I spent those mournful days beside the fire, dejected, angrily struggling against the illness which, in this bad weather, triumphed. Gloomy days: I could neither read nor work; the slightest effort made me break out into a nasty sweat; to focus my attention exhausted me; the moment I stopped controlling each breath, I began choking for air." For Proust, obviously, illness and medicine are capital subjects, which he treats with more unsparing and copious detail than the minimalist Gide. Here's a typical passage from Proust: "We went into the sickroom. Bent in a semi-circle on the bed, a creature other than my grandmother, a sort of beast that had put on her hair and crouched among her bedclothes, lay panting, whimpering, making the blankets heave with its convulsions. The eyelids were closed, and it was because they did not shut properly rather than because they opened that they disclosed a chink of eyeball, blurred, rheumy, reflecting the dimness of an organic vision and of an inward pain. All this agitation was not addressed to us, whom she neither saw nor knew." One cannot accuse Proust of long-windedness, only of an excessively detailed fascination with his subject. Whereas Gide suggests, Proust spells everything out.

But even if the committee had liked the prose, the book was much too long for a fledgling house. Gide, ever the guilty Protestant, was eager later on to assume all the blame. He claimed that he had just dipped into the book here and there and had been struck by the sordidness of the description of Aunt Léonie's medicines and offended by the peculiar mention of the "vertebrae" showing through her nearly transparent forehead. He had met Proust twenty years earlier in a salon and thought of him as no more than a right-winger and flatterer. At the end of his life Gide was still worrying about his misjudgment, asking himself, "Would I have been able to recognize right away the obvious value of Baudelaire, of Rimbaud? Wouldn't I have dismissed Lautréamont at first as a madman?"

Another member of the committee tried to absolve Gide retrospectively by making the blame collective. Jean Schlumberger wrote: "I maintain that no one, neither Gide nor Gaston nor Copeau nor I, had read the manuscript. At the most we'd all just pecked at it, here and there, just a few paragraphs in which the writing seemed unpromising. We refused the work because of its enormous size and because of Proust's reputation as a snob." Later Gallimard would turn down another French masterpiece of the century, Céline's *Journey to the End of Night*.

The extraordinary thing is that not once was Proust's faith in his writing shaken. He might wail that the book had been easy to write but was so difficult to publish. He might feel irritated that no one took him seriously enough to hear out his explanations of where the whole long work was headed or to grasp his ideas about the symphonic construction of his epic or the role of involuntary memory. No one would take the time to see that he'd written the consummate *Bildungsroman*, the apprenticeship novel in which the hero learns about painting, music, and literature from, respectively, the characters known as Elstir (based partially on Whistler), Vinteuil, and Bergotte. Nor had they read enough to see that the love of the Narrator for Albertine would echo Swann's for Odette, and that passion is always a disappointment in Proust's world and family love the only form of affection that endures. But despite his frustration, Proust remained coolly adamant that his book was something of lasting merit.

Proust made another effort. His book was submitted to a publishing house called Ollendorff. The director, a man named Humblot, replied, "I may be narrow-minded but I can't understand how a gentleman can use thirty pages to describe how he tosses and turns in his bed before falling asleep." Proust commented: "Here's a man . . . who has had in his hands 700 pages in which you can easily see that so much moral experience, thought and pain have been concentrated, not diluted, and that's the manner he uses to brush the book aside."

With marvelous resourcefulness and resilience, Proust immediately asked a friend whether Bernard Grasset would publish his book if all the expenses were paid: what today we would call "vanity publishing," except that in those days in France well-heeled authors, even those who were well-known and talented, often resorted to subsidizing their own publication—not so hard to understand in a period when even the most famous writers seldom sold more than two thousand copies of their books. Grasset, whom Proust compared to an ebony paper-cutter, so hard and sharp and efficient was he, virtually invented modern publishing in France; he was the first to resort to massive press offensives, advertising, bribing well-known personalities to launch a good word-of-mouth campaign, and so on. His "stable" would one day include Jean Giraudoux, the playwright (*The Madwoman of Chaillot*), and François Mauriac, the novelist.

Grasset agreed to publish Proust, who benefited from Grasset's knowhow, although the two men never became friendly. Perhaps they were too similar, since Proust was not only a great artist but also a genius at self-promotion, someone who showered critics with gifts, who wined and dined opinion makers, and never failed to respond to a good review with exaggerated gratitude and a bad one with pages and pages of self-justification—and more often than not an invitation to the Ritz.

IX

IF PROUST'S LAW is that you always get what you want when you no longer want it, then publication exemplified this tragic principle, since by the time Proust's book came out on November 14, 1913, the event had been completely upstaged by the great love of his life and its brutal conclusion.

Proust had met Alfred Agostinelli in 1907, when the teenage chauffeur from Monaco drove Proust through the Norman countryside, using Cabourg as their starting point. Ironically, Agostinelli worked for a Monaco-based taxi company run by Proust's first love, Jacques Bizet. Within a few months Proust had already written an essay about the almost religious exhilaration of "flying" across the countryside in an automobile—the same sort of pleasure Henry James was enjoying at the same time in Edith Wharton's luxurious car. In the essay, "Impressions of the Road in an Automobile," Proust compared his moon-faced, mustachioed young chauffeur wearing goggles and a close-fitting aviator's hat to a male pilgrim—and to a wimpled nun. The next year Agostinelli drove Proust from Cabourg to

Versailles, where Proust liked to spend every autumn in a melancholy grand hotel, the Hôtel des Réservoirs. Overcome with asthma, Proust stayed shut up in his room or played dominoes with Agostinelli and his valet, Odilon Albaret. Since he had no more need of Agostinelli, Proust dismissed him and apparently forgot him, until he resurfaced in 1913.

Agostinelli was now twenty-five, leaner, out of work, and living with a woman named Anna who he claimed was his wife (in fact they weren't married). As Proust already had his faithful servant Albaret, he didn't need another driver, but he offered Agostinelli a job as a secretary. Soon Proust and Agostinelli were spending long hours together in Proust's bedroom working on the manuscript—and Proust became deeply enamored of him. Agostinelli even moved in to Proust's apartment with Anna. Proust wrote a friend that the couple had become "an integral part of my existence." With all the exaggeration of love, Proust declared Agostinelli to be "an extraordinary being possessing perhaps the greatest intellectual gifts I've ever known!" He later told Gide that "I have letters from him which are those of a great writer." Proust's maid Céleste Albaret, married to the valet-chauffeur, said merely that he was "an unstable boy" who had "ambitions to rise above his station." Proust himself wrote in *The Fugitive*, "Certainly I'd known people with a higher intelligence. But love, boundless in its egotism, means that the beings whom we love are those whose intellectual

and moral features are for us the least objectively defined."
Everyone agreed that Anna was ugly, and Odilon Albaret
called her "the flying louse" ("ugly as a louse" is a common
French expression). She was also intensely jealous, and
Agostinelli, though he seemed to love her, cheated on her
constantly with other women. Oddly enough, it never
occurred to her to be jealous of Proust, nor did the demoni-
cally possessive Proust seem to be jealous of her. At that
time homosexual relations, especially between the classes,
were viewed benignly as a form of patronage—or weren't
focused upon at all, except when a scandal erupted; and such
scandals were never characteristic of France. Oscar Wilde
had his trial in London in 1895 and was convicted; in 1900 the
Belgian gay writer Georges Eekhoud was tried for his novel
Escal-Vigor and was acquitted; in 1902 Friedrich Alfred
Krupp committed suicide following a scandal about his
homosexuality; in 1903 Sir Hector Archibald Macdonald
shot himself; and in 1907 it seemed everyone in Germany
was accusing everyone else of "uranism" (even the chan-
cellor of Germany, for instance, brought a successful libel
suit against someone for accusing him of homosexuality;
Count Kuno von Moltke brought a similar suit against the
journalist Maximilian Harden, and lost; and the following
year Prince Eulenburg was arrested for a second time and
tried repeatedly until the collapse of his health brought an
end to all legal proceedings). In France no such scandals ever
arose, in large part because the laws dating back to 1791 (and

ratified by the penal code of 1810) had already decrimi-
nalized sodomy—laws briefly reinstated only under the
Vichy regime during World War II.

Even more important, a "patronage" sort of homosexuality in which an older, richer gay man helped along in his
career a younger, poorer, usually heterosexual man was
virtually an institution in Latin countries until the 1950s,
when growing prosperity and unsupervised heterosexual
dating at an earlier age did away with the foundations of
such a practice. But in Proust's day this sort of quasi-sexual
patronage, far from seeming exploitive, was actually considered to be charitable and generous. Proust's sexual tastes
changed over time from an attraction to gay artistic peers
(such as Reynaldo Hahn and Lucien Daudet) to working-
class heterosexuals such as Agostinelli and, subsequently,
Henri Rochat, a waiter at the Ritz—a change that, of
course, would make him intensely unhappy.

Agostinelli, besides being linked to the ugly, jealous
Anna, had a sister who was the mistress of the baron
Duquesne, a brother who was a chauffeur, a half-brother
who worked as a hotel waiter, and a demanding father.
Alfred apparently sent money to all of them, which he
earned by gouging Monsieur Proust (at one point Proust
sold some Royal Dutch stocks worth twenty thousand dollars in today's money and wired it all to Agostinelli). In a
letter to his banker Proust wearily remarked, "When one
loves not members of society but people more or less poor,
these sufferings over love usually double one's considerable

financial problems." He thought that it was a shame he couldn't fall in love with a member of his own class, since it would have cost him a great deal less money.

Proust was certainly in love, to the point that once he and his entourage had arrived in Cabourg in 1913 for the whole summer, after a few days he suddenly decided that he had to return to Paris instantly in order to be near some mysterious woman. The "woman," in fact, was Agostinelli himself, who had to drive Proust back to the capital, a sudden whim that gave Proust a few precious days alone with his beloved and removed the young man from the presence of a new woman he'd just met at Cabourg and whom he had begun to court. In *Remembrance of Things Past* the Narrator, worried that Albertine is about to take up with Vinteuil's lesbian daughter and her friend, invents an amorous pretext for dashing back from Balbec to Paris with Albertine. Proust knew perfectly well that he was only irritating Agostinelli, but his jealousy was stronger than his wisdom. He cut his beard, hoping to please his beloved, but to no avail. As he'd told friends more than once, he was better at giving advice in love than following it himself. His burning, constant jealousy inspired him in late August 1913 to add a few new details to his novel: "little facts that are very important for tightening the knots of jealousy around poor Swann." Proust knew that all he had to offer Agostinelli was money, but to the extent that his bribes to the young man were becoming larger and larger, the sooner was he giving Agostinelli the means to defect.

Especially since Agostinelli preferred adventure to wealth. He had been thrilled by the first automobiles, but now, on the eve of the coming war, he was drawn to aviation. Proust offered to pay for flying lessons in the Paris region (the Narrator accompanies the excited Albertine to all the flying fields around Paris). Proust made a substantial down payment for lessons in a school outside Paris, but then suddenly Agostinelli bolted.

In all, Agostinelli lived with Proust only from the beginning of 1913 to the morning of December 1, when he and Anna left without explanation while Proust slept. In fact he'd gone to Antibes, near his native Monaco. Why did he leave? To escape Proust's constant jealous interrogations? Or because Anna disliked Paris? Sadly, ironically, Agostinelli registered at his new flight school under the pseudonym of "Marcel Swann." Why did he even need a pseudonym? To avoid being located by the jealous monster (and his literary counterpart) that the compound fictional name invoked?

A devastated Proust asked his old secretary Albert Nahmias if he knew the address of a policeman who could "follow" someone—a private eye, in other words. Proust also wrote Agostinelli's father, promising him a handsome monthly salary if he could convince his son to return to Paris—only till April (Proust apparently knew he could not expect too much even in the best of scenarios). Nahmias himself was dispatched to Antibes and instructed to offer Agostinelli money, threats, ultimatums, bribes. In a generous mood, Proust ordered Agostinelli an airplane (just as the Narrator tries to lure Albertine back by offering her a yacht). In a vindictive mood Proust wrote Agostinelli, "If ever ill fortune decrees that you have an airplane accident, you can make it clear to your wife that she will find in me neither a protector, nor a friend, nor a source of money."

Proust's novel *Swann's Way* was published in November 1913, but his year of suffering with Agostinelli and—after December 1 and the young man's departure—his even greater agony of living without him meant that he took no pleasure at all in the long-awaited artistic event, even if the book received much praise, including a letter from the writer Francis Jammes comparing Proust to Shakespeare, Balzac, and Tacitus. When Proust, confounding literature and his miserable life, received a mixed review a few days after Agostinelli's flight, he wrote Cocteau, "I've seen my novel reflected in it as in a mirror counselling suicide." To an unknown fan, Proust wrote, "Right now I'm living through the most painful moment of my life after the death of my mother. And the pleasure that you are good enough to say my book has brought you, it does not at all procure for me." In the early spring, however, Agostinelli began to drop occasional notes to Proust; perhaps he feared that his money might someday run out. Being back in touch with his beloved, no matter what Agostinelli's motives were, over-joyed Proust.

And then suddenly the world came to an end. On May 30, 1914, after two months of lessons, Agostinelli went out on his second solo flight. Against his teacher's advice he flew out over the Mediterranean and then, while making a low-altitude turn, crashed into the water. He couldn't swim. He waved frantically while clinging to the wreckage, then sank with it and drowned. A great deal of money was found on his body, which he kept with him all the time since he couldn't trust his greedy family members not to steal it.

Proust was devastated. He wrote Reynaldo Hahn, "I truly loved Alfred. It's not enough to say I loved him, I adored him. And I don't know why I write that in the past tense since I still love him." In spite of his earlier nasty letters to Agostinelli, Proust took in Anna, tried to console her and attempted to be brave for her sake; he also helped her start a new life. He was unable to work. In June 1914, when Proust began to receive the typeset pages for his second volume, he wrote André Gide, "Since the death of my poor friend I haven't had the courage to open even one of the packages of proofs that Grasset sends me every day." The following November Proust wrote Lucien Daudet that he was so upset that "each time I get into a taxi I know what it's like to wish with all my heart that the approaching bus might crush me."

As it turned out, that second volume he was supposed to be correcting would not be published until five years later, in a very different form and under the aegis of a different publishing house. What Proust could not have predicted when he began *Remembrance of Things Past* were two catastrophes that would completely change the shape of his book: the First World War, which broke out in 1914, and the death of Agostinelli. German air attacks on Paris became an important backdrop for the later action of the book, just as the frontline conflict kills some of the major characters and the upheaval of the war radically metamorphoses the old social order, by ruining some of the old aristocratic families and advancing certain middle-class people to positions of prominence. Proust writes movingly of the sight of a nearly deserted Paris in 1914 under the "unchanged antique splendor of a moon cruelly, mysteriously serene, which poured the useless beauty of its light on monuments that were still intact."

Even more crucially, the loss of Agostinelli led to the elevation of Albertine to the level of principal character, to the amplification of *Within a Budding Grove* as a separate volume, replete with scenes of the young girls who surround Albertine, and to the invention of the two volumes devoted entirely to Albertine's life with the Narrator, flight, and death, *The Captive* and *The Fugitive*. Rather than distorting the proportions of the whole book, as some critics have complained, the introduction of Albertine actually fills an immense void, "since little dalliances without importance and fleeting flirtations are replaced by the violent, tragic grandeur of a Racinian passion," as Proust's best and most recent biographer, Jean-Yves Tadié, writes. "And a new theme will be introduced, which was lacking in the original plans if not in *Pleasures and Days*, the theme of female homosexuality: Gomorrah will now be a true adjunct to Sodom." In the eight years following Agostinelli's death Proust's book doubled in volume.

La Nouvelle Revue Française realized the mistake that had been made in rejecting *Swann's Way*. Jacques Rivière, a sickly, brilliant young man whom Proust came to consider the best critic of his generation, was the first of the *NRF* team to read the published book all the way through and to announce to his colleagues their disastrous oversight. André Gide wrote to Proust in 1914, "The refusal of this book will remain the most serious mistake of the N.R.F.— and (since I'm ashamed to be largely responsible) one of the most bitter regrets and causes of remorse in my life."

But Proust graciously responded, "I've often felt that certain great pleasures require that we first must be deprived of a pleasure of a lesser sort. . . ." The *NRF* was more than a commercial venture; it was a consecration by Proust's peers. But he could not bring himself to break with Grasset right away, out of timidity and halfhearted loyalty, and only after many complex maneuverings did he change from one house to the other. Even so, no books were being published during the war, and Proust had to wait until 1919 for the appearance in print of *Within a Budding Grove*.

The only compensation Proust found for the loss of Agostinelli was in Ernst Forssgren, a six-foot-four blond Swedish Adonis, whom he engaged as a valet and soon promoted to the status of secretary. He took Forssgren off with him in 1914 for one last season at Cabourg, when the two men would spend hours playing easy card games and chatting. Proust said to him, "Ernst, in all my life I've never known a person I loved as much as I love you," a declaration he would make to many men over the years. But nothing could lighten the melancholy that had descended over Proust and his whole world. Suddenly, the hotel was converted into a hospital, Proust limped back to Paris after a dreadful asthma crisis, and Forssgren, afraid that he might be drafted into the Swedish army, emigrated to the United States.

X

Proust's war years were devoted to his work. He would fearlessly travel across the city in search of a detail and would think nothing of waking up a family after midnight in order to quiz the members about an ancient anecdote or to visit the headwaiter at the Ritz in order to go over a piece of time-honored gossip. He wrote literally thousands of letters, many of them to obtain precise information about a certain dress worn in the 1890s or a famous witticism uttered during the Belle Epoque.

But he was not entirely immersed in the happier past. He kept careful track of the war as it unfolded all around him. His principal worry was that despite his terrible health he might be called up for military service, and he was not declared unfit until well into the war. He was also stunned by the deaths of his friends, especially that of Bertrand de Fénelon, who was killed in battle on December 17, 1914. In 1917 Emmanuel Bibesco, afflicted with a terminal disease, committed suicide. Many other friends died in the war.

His home life has been unforgettably rendered by his

maid, Céleste Albaret, in her book of "as told to" memoirs, *Monsieur Proust*. She recounts how after her husband went off to war, she was Proust's sole servant, and how she adapted herself to Proust's schedule. She would mother Proust all night long, bringing him things to drink or eat, filling his hot-water bottles, sometimes preparing him for his rare midnight sorties, since he was afraid to go out any earlier, before the day's dust had settled. If he did go out, he would give Céleste a full report on what the ladies wore, who was cheating on whom, how they were related to the people he'd known in his youth, and so on. He never asked her to sit but kept her standing for hours as he excitedly recited his impressions from his bed. She would then retire around eight or nine in the morning and awaken around two in the afternoon.

Céleste's great anxiety was Proust's morning (or afternoon) coffee. It had to be ready the moment he rang for it, but the preparation took at least half an hour, since he liked the water to be dripped, drop by drop, through the grounds, in order to produce the thickest, strongest possible "essence" of coffee. Nor could he bear for it to be reheated, which he could detect right away by the burned taste; if Proust did not ring soon after the coffee was ready, she would have to pour it out and start the whole process all over again. Only in her bedroom and in the kitchen were the curtains ever opened. Daylight never penetrated into the other rooms. Nor could the windows be opened to air the apartment until the master went out, which was never

before ten at night. At the same time she was at last allowed
to do the housework and make up the master's bed.

When she complained to Proust that he never let her go
to mass on Sunday, he replied very sweetly, "Céleste, do
you know that you are doing something far more noble and
far greater than going to mass? You're giving your time to
care for a sick man. That's infinitely finer." And yet he cared
for her genuinely, too, showering her with gifts, taking her
education in hand, and chiding her when she did embroi-
dery instead of reading. Only his mother and Céleste ever
gave him the unconditional love that he expected. At
Cabourg Proust would knock on the wall between their
rooms to summon Céleste, just as the Narrator knocks to
call his feeble, adoring grandmother. Céleste stayed with
Proust until the end of his life. She went so far in her loyalty
as to deny his homosexuality altogether when she was
quizzed by biographers later.

Nevertheless, Céleste Albaret did not hesitate to recount
that during the war Proust visited (for the purposes of
"research," as she put it) a male brothel for homosexuals,
run by Albert Le Cuziat, a former valet in princely house-
holds who not only catered to the most bizarre tastes of
his rich clientele but also knew their lineages by heart.
Proust consulted him often for anecdotes he could use in
Sodom and Gomorrah. Proust helped Le Cuziat pay for the
building where his establishment was housed and, more
shockingly, even gave some of his parents' furniture to be
used in this hotbed of homosexual prostitution—perhaps

his most extreme act of profanation, given the cult he had established around the memory of his mother and father. One might point out that at about the same time Proust gave his father's clothes to the deceased Alfred Agostinelli's brother, Emile—again a profanation, considering how much Dr. Proust would have hated having his things worn by someone from the family of his son's lover.

According to the German (and heterosexual) essayist Walter Benjamin—who went on a "field trip" to the brothel in 1930 with the weird writer Maurice Sachs (a Jewish homosexual who collaborated with the Nazis during the war)—the story was still circulating at the bordello that Proust had been known as "the rat man." Sachs—a witness more flamboyant than reliable—wrote that Proust had a live rat brought to him in a cage and stabbed to death with hat pins as he watched with lust and fear. Proust was afraid of rats and mice—he even wrote a friend during the war that he was more afraid of rats than of bombs. The Narrator dreams that his parents have become white mice in a cage, covered with pustules.

Proust told Gide that in order to achieve an orgasm he needed to bring together many unusual elements. Voyeurism and masturbation seem to have been his two principal erotic modes, at least with casual partners. And in the memoirs of several writers who knew him the story is related that Proust profaned the photos of his mother during sex by spitting on them or insulting them (of course Proust himself never mentioned such a thing, if it occurred). Certainly this possibility takes on some credibility, however, through the dozens of strange references to photos in Proust's work, including the insults hurled at Vinteuil's portrait by his daughter's lesbian girlfriend just before the two women collapse in a frenzy of lust. Proust's insistence that friends send him signed photographic portraits acquires a lurid gleam given what we know about his use of these pictures, at least in his imagination. Proust was also extremely alert to every possibility of defilement in general, and in one letter he assures a correspondent that he had no evil thoughts, for instance, when he mentioned the "pleasure" of entering a church—a double meaning that would occur to no one else.

All of these bits of evidence conspire to suggest that Proust's sexuality depended on defiling sacred objects, at least as a way of kick-starting it. For instance, the baron de Charlus (to whom Proust quite openly assigned many of his own characteristics) becomes strangely excited when he remarks to the Narrator about his Jewish friend Bloch:

> "Perhaps you could ask your friend to allow me to attend some great festival in the Temple, a circumcision, or some Hebrew chants . . . You might perhaps arrange that, and even some comic exhibitions. For instance a contest between your friend and his father, in which he would smite him as David smote Goliath. That would make quite an amusing farce. He might even, while he was about it, give his hag . . . of a mother a good thrashing. That would be an excellent show, and would not be unpleasing to us,

eh, my young friend, since we like exotic spectacles, and to thrash that non-European creature would be giving a well-earned punishment to an old cow. . . ."

In 1917 and 1918 Proust, as though tempted for a last time by worldly pleasure, once more went out frequently, mainly to the Ritz, where he would dine alone, very late, or with an amusing, nonstop raconteur—the society priest Abbé Mugnier, or Walter Berry, Edith Wharton's American lover, or the prince de Polignac (whose wife was the American sewing-machine heiress Winnaretta Singer). He went out so often because he had found in the Ritz a populous, luxurious, congenial salon, a place where he was cosseted by the waiters and could dine even after midnight. The headwaiter, Olivier Dabescat, knew everyone in high society and supplied Proust with dozens of anecdotes for his book. Proust was also bewitched by a young couple, the princesse Soutzo and her lover, the talented writer Paul Morand; their physical beauty and exquisite polish excited him, and he joined them frequently at the Ritz for dinner or a chamber music recital. In 1918 Proust was giving as many as three dinner parties a week at the Ritz.

In order to find the energy for these sorties—and for his marathon sessions of writing and correcting proofs—Proust abused stimulants such as adrenaline and caffeine, which of course led to the necessity of taking calming substances such as opium at bedtime. His already fragile health was further weakened through these excesses, and he began to suffer from dizzy spells that caused him to fall down, even several times in a day, and to undergo passing attacks of aphasia—when he was unable to recall a word, or if he knew it, to pronounce it.

Despite his deteriorating health and arduous work schedule, Proust was now forced to find new lodgings. His aunt, who owned his building, sold it to a bank and ousted her nephew; he found temporary refuge in the noisy, dusty house of the famous actress Réjane (one of the originals for Proust's character the actress Berma) on the rue Laurent-Pichat before taking a permanent place at 44 rue Hamelin. Even in the midst of these wrenching dislocations, Proust kept his sense of humor. For instance, he wrote his best friend, Madame Straus, that his aunt had just sent him "a masterpiece" of a letter in which she said she preferred the "sweet name of aunt to that of owner" and that now that she had sold the building out from under her sick nephew they would be able to discuss "literature and not domestic matters."

At the end of June 1919, now that the war was over, Gallimard was at last able to bring out three of Proust's books: a reissue of *Swann's Way*, the first-ever publication of *Within a Budding Grove*, and a collection of Proust's pastiches and other short pieces, many of them written fifteen or even twenty years earlier. By the end of the year Proust had received France's most prestigious literary award, the

Goncourt Prize, for *Within a Budding Grove*, although not without actively courting the judges with expensive presents and fine meals. And not without controversy. The vote was just six to four in Proust's favor; a noisy faction of the public and press denounced the decision, which they saw as the coronation of an invalid who lived in the past ("a talent from beyond the tomb," as one journalist put it) and had never fought in the war. Proust was considered far less deserving than Roland Dorgelès, who had written a stirring, patriotic war epic, *The Wooden Crosses* (later made into a successful French film in the 1930s).

On the Right, a spokesman for the war veterans denounced Proust's election with fire and scorn. Leftists pointed out that Proust had garnered the vote of Léon Daudet, an old friend (as the older brother of Lucien) and a co-founder, along with the writer Charles Maurras, of the anti-Semitic, jingoistic political party Action Française. No matter that Proust himself had been a Dreyfusard at a time when Léon was vigorously anti-Dreyfusard. No matter that Proust had quite recently taken a stand against a chauvinist manifesto signed by Maurras (among others) calling for an "intellectual federation" under the aegis of France, the "guardian of all civilization," a concept that Proust dismissed as sloppy thinking, since he believed the arts and sciences should never be dragooned into serving any political or national purpose. Now that Proust's reputation as a serious novelist was growing, even his old friends listened to him with a new seriousness. He was no longer the chronicler of society events but a philosophical, even universal, novelist.

But the victory was not yet secure. His critics dismissed his book as disorganized childhood and adolescent memories—formless, plotless, endless. Since Proust himself knew how the whole epic turned out, he was impatient for Gallimard to rush the later volumes into print. He was convinced that once critics had the entire seven volumes in hand they would see the overall design. The apparently meandering prologue to the whole epic, "Combray," for instance, is actually something like a strict overture to an opera, in the sense that it announces and compresses all the successive themes. Thus the two paths, or "ways," the Méséglise way (also known as Swann's way) and the Guermantes way, which seem to the Narrator as a child to be two entirely different itineraries leading in opposite directions, are revealed in the very last volume, *Time Regained,* to be joined—in fact, to be the same path. The adult narrator learns about this surprising unity from Swann's daughter Gilberte, who herself has married a Guermantes relative, Robert de Saint-Loup. The heraldic weight of the Guermantes name is first touched on in "Combray," as is the theme of illness (real and imaginary), snobbism, the difference between family love and romantic passion, the power of reading to bewitch, and so on. Developing themes and recurring characters spanning the whole long arc of the seven books give it an architectural solidity which casual readers of the first two volumes could not have suspected.

Similarly, the theme of involuntary memory, announced in "Combray" by the madeleine and the realization that taste and smell alone bear "the vast structure of recollection," is not fully worked out until *Time Regained*, when three successive sensations awaken three involuntary memories—and the past is brilliantly, eternally recaptured and made available as material for literature. Two uneven paving stones in the Guermantes' courtyard bring back a flood of memories about two similar stones in St. Mark's church in Venice. Later, the sound of a spoon chiming on a plate reminds the Narrator of the noise of a hammer on the metal wheel of a train, heard years earlier when his train had stopped in the woods. Finally, a stiff napkin makes the Narrator recall the starchy towel he'd dried off with when he was a boy, during his first visit to Balbec.

In analyzing the joy that these memories bring him, Proust realizes that at the time they occurred he was unable to bring his imagination to bear on the experiences, the imagination "which was the only organ that I possessed for the enjoyment of beauty. . . ." Now, however, involuntary memory allowed the recollected experiences "to be mirrored at one and the same time in the past, so that my imagination was permitted to savor it, and in the present, where the actual shock to my senses of the noise, the touch of the linen napkin, or whatever it might be, had added to the dreams of the imagination the concept of 'existence' which they usually lack, and through this subterfuge had made it possible for my being to secure, to isolate, to immobilize—for a moment brief as a flash of lightning—what normally it never apprehends: a fragment of time in the pure state."

Proust always claimed that he had a bad memory and that, besides, a carefully reconstructed recollection, prompted by photos or shared reminiscences, was invariably color-less. Only an involuntary memory, triggered by a taste or smell or other sensation, could erase the passage of time and restore a past experience in its first, full effulgence. Proust was anti-intellectual and convinced that the domain of art, which is recollected experience, can never be tapped through reasoning or method alone; it must be delivered to us, fresh and vivid, through a process beyond the control of the intellect or willpower. Paradoxically, if Proust was anti-intellectual he was also profoundly philosophical, in that what he sought was not the accidents but the essence of any past event. Involuntary memory, by definition anti-intellectual, nevertheless refines away all the unnecessary details of a forgotten moment and retains only its un-adorned core.

Proust, who through ill health was forced to lie utterly still in bed for hours on end meditating on his life, was natu-rally predisposed to turning the people he knew and the adventures he lived through into glowing legends. Because he was so determined to disguise his own homosexuality, he was forced to transpose recalled experiences with men into beguiling tales of the Narrator's passion for women. This elaborate game of encoding is the creative half of Proust's effort, the invention added to the data provided by involuntary memory. But as in the case of a good Method actor who builds even the most bizarre characterization on his own concrete and personal sense memories, in the same way Proust's strategies of disguise and transposition must still begin and end with a highly specific recollection of his own feelings and sensations. In that sense, involuntary memories represent the truth in Proust's process of composition, the bare face that he must later paint with invention.

Perhaps the theory of the primacy of involuntary memory appeals to readers because it assures us that nothing is ever truly forgotten and that art is nothing but the accumulation of memories. This utterly democratic view that we are all novelists who have been handed by destiny one big book, the story of our lives, appeals to anyone who has ever felt the tug towards self-expression but has feared not being skilled enough to get his feelings down. Of course what Proust leaves out of the equation are three essential things: the fact that he happened to live at one of the highpoints of culture and civilization (if not of literary creation); his natural gifts of eloquence, analysis of psychology, and assimilation of information; and finally his willingness to sacrifice his life to his art. Involuntary memory, without the addition of such gifts and happy circumstances, would probably not be much of a guarantee of artistic excellence. Since Proust possessed such powers in profusion, he could afford to dismiss their importance.

XI

THE INITIAL ATTACKS on Proust were quickly forgotten and the long, slow process of artistic canonization began, with translations into several languages under way and dithyrambic essays rushing into print. But the full impact of Proust's vision was not realized until 1927 and the publication of the last volume of his massive work—five years after his death. He died in 1922, after *The Guermantes Way* and *Sodom and Gomorrah* had been published, but before the publication of *The Captive* in 1923, *The Fugitive* in 1925, and *Time Regained* in 1927 (as well as *Jean Santeuil* in 1952, *Contre Sainte-Beuve* in 1954, and all twenty-one volumes of his letters, brought out between 1970 and 1993).

In the summer of 1918, as the war was approaching its end, Proust was still far from the end of the onerous task he'd set himself. Nor had desire for love or at least male companionship died away. He became enamored of a waiter at the Ritz named Henri Rochat, a handsome Swiss who wanted to be a painter. Soon after Proust met him he insisted that Rochat serve him every time he dined at the

Ritz. Then he began to shower him with gifts, especially expensive clothes. As in the days of Agostinelli, Proust was again making vague references in letters to friends of his "great moral grief," which he was convinced would poison every instant of his life and bring about his death. To his exasperated banker Proust confessed that he had spent about forty thousand dollars on the young person. When the banker suggested that Proust safeguard his remaining fortune (which he had reduced by roughly 25 percent through reckless spending and bad investments) by placing it in such a way that he could not touch the capital, Proust loftily replied that love is a cruel passion that renders life cheap.

Rochat seldom left Proust's apartment, where he had a room of his own. He spent most of the day by himself, painting. In *The Captive* the Narrator writes that "Albertine's paintings, the captive's touching distractions, moved me so much that I complimented her on them." What researchers have figured out in recent years is that Proust wrote first *The Fugitive*, soon after Agostinelli's departure and death, while the material was still vivid in his mind and a weight on his heart, whereas he elaborated *The Captive* later, even though the book actually precedes *The Fugitive* in the published sequence. Why? Simply because the main inspiration for the Albertine of *The Captive* is Henri Rochat, not Alfred Agostinelli. It was Rochat who lived in his own room, solitary and self-sufficient, in Proust's gloomy apartment, whereas Agostinelli had lived with his wife and only briefly under Proust's roof. Accordingly, *The Captive*, which had been sketched out as early as 1916, doubled in size during the two years Rochat lived with Proust.

The simple act of "possessing" another human being is something that Proust describes in *The Captive* with depth and sweetness ("For the possession of what we love is an even greater joy than love itself," he writes). About Albertine the Narrator says:

> . . . And just as people pay a hundred francs a day for a room at the Grand Hotel at Balbec in order to breathe the sea air, I felt it to be quite natural that I should spend more than that on her, since I had her breath upon my cheek, between my lips which I laid half-open upon hers, through which her life flowed against my tongue.

> But this pleasure of seeing her sleep, which was as sweet to me as that of feeling her live, was cut short by another pleasure, that of seeing her wake. It was, carried to a more profound and more mysterious degree, the same pleasure as I felt in having her under my roof. . . .

Interestingly, it is only in this passage that the Narrator ever calls himself "Marcel," and then only provisionally. When Albertine awakens she says:

> "My—" or "My darling—" followed by my Christian name which, if we give the narrator the same name as the author of this book, would be "My Marcel," or "My darling Marcel."

Soon Rochat's presence—so cool and self-sufficient, so obviously dedicated to milking his master—began to annoy

Proust, who sought to get rid of him. He complained to Madame Straus that he had embarked on a romantic affair "without a way out, without joy and constantly involving fatigue, suffering and absurd expenses." In 1919 Proust accompanied him to the train station, so eager was he to see him off. Proust had arranged for his passport and even a job possibility in Switzerland, but all too soon Rochat returned to Paris and moved back in with Proust ("He came to ask me for a hospitality that I could not refuse him but that poisons my existence," Proust wrote a friend). Only at the end of May 1921 did Proust finally convince Rochat to leave for Buenos Aires and a bank job, though no one has ever been able to find a trace of him in Argentina. In leaving, Rochat abandoned his fiancée, just as the handsome, perfidious violinist Morel jilts his fiancée, Jupien's niece. When the demanding young "captive" finally flew the coop, all Proust could say to his maid was, "At last, Céleste, here we are, nice and peaceful."

In January 1920, Proust had published in *La Nouvelle Revue Française* one of his most striking literary essays, devoted to Flaubert's style. He was responding to a recent article that had charged Flaubert with being a bad writer. Proust was quick to admit that Flaubert lacked the ability to invent metaphors ("I believe that metaphor alone can give a sort of eternity to style, and in all of Flaubert there is perhaps not one fine metaphor"). But he defended Flaubert's innovative use of verb tenses, even his mournful sequence of events and gray vocabulary. Perhaps he saw Flaubert as his opposite, for surely no one ever discovered more beautiful and lasting ("eternal") metaphors than Proust. In discussing the writer in *Time Regained*, Proust, echoing Baudelaire's theory of correspondences, tells us, "He can describe a scene by describing one after another the innumerable objects which at a given moment were present at a particular place, but truth will be obtained by him only when he takes two different objects, states the connection between them. . . . Truth—and life too—can be attained by us only when, by comparing a quality common to two sensations, we succeed in extracting their common essence and in reuniting them to each other within a metaphor, liberated from the contingencies of time." Proust's own prose is replete with such liberating metaphors, as when he compares the sleeping Albertine to a pomegranate, bland and featureless on the outside but guarding all her bejeweled, treacherous thoughts within, or as when he likens the diners at Belleville to solar systems and the waiters to fleeting comets, or as when Swann, painfully in love, hears the first stirrings of the "little theme," the anthem of his love for Odette, as the disguised arrival of a goddess.

In the spring of 1921, Proust, weak and more and more subject to dizzy spells, made one of his last outings in order to see a Vermeer painting, *The View of Delft,* in an exhibition at the Jeu de Paume. He used the same occasion when he came to write about the death of the character Bergotte, the novelist, who loses consciousness after looking at the little patch of yellow in the celebrated canvas. Indeed, on the night before he died Proust dictated a last sentence, "There is a Chinese patience in Vermeer's craft." Proust could sense that his own death would not be long in coming, and he wrote Francis Jammes, "In your prayers to Saint Joseph ask him to give me a death that will be more gentle than my life has been."

In May 1921 *Sodom and Gomorrah* went on sale, and Proust was almost disappointed by the lack of scandal. Perhaps his olympian style, with its coolness and philosophical compulsion to find general truths even in the most exotic (and trashy) particulars, tranquilized his readers' moralistic responses. To be sure, almost no one who did not know him thought that Proust himself was homosexual. The Narrator is one of the few unambiguous heterosexuals in the book; almost all the other characters turn out to be gay. After Proust's death several essays congratulated him on his "courage" in braving such disgusting corners of experience, as though Proust were a moral Jean-Henri Fabre—the pioneering entomologist—and his homosexual characters were insects.

One of his few acquaintances who was not happy with the ugly picture Proust drew of homosexuals was Gide, who in 1911 had already published anonymously his groundbreaking defense of homosexuality, *Corydon*, which he would reissue under his own name in 1924. Gide came twice in May 1921 to Proust's bedside to discuss "uranism." According to Gide's journal, "he said he had never loved women except spiritually and had never known love except with men." When, during the second visit, Gide reproached him for his negative picture of homosexuality, Proust said that he had transposed to the female characters all his homosexual memories that were tender and charming and so had been left with nothing but grotesque details for his homosexual characters. Perhaps he was only trying to appease and charm the indignant Gide, for elsewhere Proust defended his grotesque vision of "inverts" by arguing that whereas homosexuality may have been treated as natural in pagan times, in the Christian era it had been so persecuted that the only gays who'd survived had been invalids impossible to cure.

The comte de Montesquiou, who had good reason to hate Proust for his portrait under the guise of the baron de Charlus, let his former protégé off lightly, pretending to recognize in Charlus only features of Balzac's character Vautrin and the contemporary homosexual the baron de Doasan. Privately, however, Montesquiou wrote a friend that he'd gone to bed sick from the publication of books that had "overwhelmed" him. He died at the end of 1921 from uremia, estranged from all his old friends and relatives because of his bilious fits of rage and general imperiousness. Everyone worried about his memoirs, which were to be published posthumously. The book, however, turned out to be a monument to vanity but fairly innocuous in its accounts of other people. His cousin the comtesse Greffulhe found it boring, saying, "It's not quite what one expects of a dead man."

In September 1922 Proust's health began to deteriorate rapidly, but on the eighteenth he still plucked up the courage to go to a hotel where his former Swedish valet, Forssgren, was to grant him an assignation. Proust waited in vain from eleven in the evening till three in the morning at the Hôtel Riviera. When Proust died soon after, his brother, Robert, asked, "What person could have been so dear to him that he would knowingly have sacrificed his health to him?"

Proust had developed pneumonia, which went untreated and turned into bronchitis and finally an abscess on the lungs. For a year he had been speaking of his own death; perhaps he was proud that he had hung on so long, to fifty-one, the age at which his prolific predecessor Balzac had died. On the morning of November 18, 1922, Proust saw a fat woman in black whom no one else could see, though Céleste dutifully promised to chase her away. Robert Proust bled him (the common treatment for lowering a fever) by applying suction cups to his back, but to no effect save for the extra pain caused by this procedure. Then, between five and six in the evening, Proust died. The American surrealist Man Ray photographed him, the society priest Mugnier prayed, and two painters drew his inanimate features. Four days later Marcel Proust was buried at Père-Lachaise, where he lies under black marble with other members of his family. The magisterial father, Professor Proust, who died long before his ne'er-do-well son began to publish his masterpiece, might have been surprised to see that the most prominent name on the monument is not "Adrien" but rather "Marcel."

No matter how strange Proust's life might have been, it has been subsumed, as he hoped, into the radiant vision of it that he presented in his writing. Nevertheless, the intensely intimate (if not always personal) quality of Proust's novel makes him more and more popular in this age of memoirs. Whereas other modernists (Stein, Joyce, Pound) rejected confession in favor of formal experiment, Proust was a literary cyclops, if that means he was a creature with a single great "I" at the center of his consciousness (no matter that the first-person Narrator is only occasionally the literal Marcel Proust). Every page of Proust is the transcript of a mind thinking—not the pell-mell stream of consciousness of a Molly Bloom or a Stephen Dedalus, each a dramatic character with a unique vocabulary and an individuating range of preoccupations, but rather the fully orchestrated, ceaseless, and disciplined ruminations of one mind, one voice: the sovereign intellect.

Proust may be more available to readers today than in the past because as his life recedes in time and the history of his period goes out of focus, he is read more as a fabulist than a chronicler, as a maker of myths rather than the valedictorian of the Belle Epoque. Under this new dispensation, Proust emerges as the supreme symphonist of the spirit. We no longer measure his accounts against a reality we know. Instead, we read his fables of caste and lust, of family virtue and social vice, of the depredations of jealousy and the consolations of art not as reports but as fairy tales. He is our Scheherazade.

Of course Proust is also popular because he writes about glamour—rich people, nobles, artists. And he wrote about love. It doesn't seem to matter that he came to despise love, that he exploded it, reduced it to its shabbiest, most mechanical, even hydraulic terms, by which I mean he not only demystified love, he also dehumanized it, turning it into something merely Pavlovian. The love Swann feels for Odette is in no way a tribute to her charms or her soul. In fact, Swann knows perfectly well that her charms are fading and that her soul is banal. Moreover, as he says to himself in the last sentence of "Swann in Love": "To think that I've wasted years of my life, that I've longed to die, that I've experienced my greatest love, for a woman who didn't appeal to me, who wasn't even my type!"

Modern readers are responsive to Proust's tireless and brilliant analyses of love because we, too, no longer take love for granted. Readers today are always making the personal public, the intimate political, the instinctual philosophical.

Proust may have attacked love, but he did know a lot about it. Like us, he took nothing for granted. He was not on smug, cozy terms with his own experience. We read Proust because he knows so much about the links between childhood anguish and adult passion. We read Proust because, despite his intelligence, he holds reasoned evaluations in contempt and knows that only the gnarled knowledge that suffering brings us is of any real use. We read Proust because he knows that in the terminal stage of passion we no longer love the beloved; the object of our love has been overshadowed by love itself: "And this malady which Swann's love had become had so proliferated, was so closely interwoven with all his habits, with all his actions, with his thoughts, his health, his sleep, his life, even with what he hoped for after his death, was so utterly inseparable from him, that it would have been impossible to eradicate it without almost entirely destroying him; as surgeons say, his love was no longer operable."

Proust may be telling us that love is a chimera, a projection of rich fantasies onto an indifferent, certainly mysterious surface, but nevertheless those fantasies are undeniably beautiful, intimations of paradise—the artificial paradise of art. I doubt whether many readers could ever be content with Proust's rejection of rustling, wounded life in favor of frozen, immobile art; but his powerful vision of impermanence certainly does speak to us. The rise and fall of individual loves on the small scale and of entire social classes on the grand, the constant revolution of sentiments and status, is a subject Proust rehearsed and we've realized. Proust is the first contemporary writer of the twentieth century, for he was the first to describe the permanent instability of our times.

BIBLIOGRAPHY

WORKS BY PROUST

In Search of Lost Time (Modern Library, 1993), in six volumes (volume 5 contains both *The Captive* and *The Fugitive*, and volume 6 contains both *Time Regained* and an extensive guide to Proust). In addition, every volume ends with a plot synopsis. This is the original translation by C. K. Scott Moncrieff, later doctored by Terence Kilmartin before it was extensively revised by D. J. Enright. Proust's seven-volume novel, *A la Recherche du temps perdu,* was first called in English in Moncrieff's version *Remembrance of Things Past* before it was retranslated, more literally, under the present title. The first volume, *Swann's Way,* first appeared in the Modern Library in 1928, and the last volume, *Time Regained,* was not published by the Modern Library until 1951 (under the title *The Past Recaptured*).

Penguin Books has commissioned a new annotated translation of *In Search of Lost Time*, due to be published in 2001. An announcement from Penguin reads: "As part of the translation process we have opened the Web pages to invite ideas and suggestions from interested Proustians around the world. Suggestions can range from particular points of translation to a wider consideration of the whole question of forms of English appropriate to a twentieth-century [*sic*] translation. . . . All e-mail will be read by the General Editor, Christopher Prendergast, at whose discretion comments will be posted to the Proust Bulletin Board. www.penguin.co.uk/proust."

For French readers, the best edition is the relatively cheap current paperback edition in Folio (Gallimard). Each volume benefits from the editing of the carefully annotated (and expensive) Pléiade edition published by Gallimard in four hardcover volumes between 1987 and 1989, meticulously edited by Proust's greatest biographer, Jean-Yves Tadié. Each Folio volume is introduced by a different scholar and contains a short bibliography, extensive notes, and a brief plot summary.

Jean Santeuil, first published in France only in 1952, appeared in an English translation by Gerard Hopkins three years later. It is still published by Penguin. Proust's stories *Les Plaisirs et les jours*, first published in French in 1896, can be found in English as *Pleasures and Regrets*, translated by Louise Varèse. Proust's *Contre Sainte-Beuve* first appeared in 1954, but the Pléiade edition of 1971, edited by Pierre Clarac, is a radically different text, organized out of Proust's fragments according to quite different principles. This later and better version was published in English by Penguin in 1988, translated by John Sturrock, who also wrote the informative introduction. This volume in English also contains many of Proust's most important literary essays, including studies of Flaubert's style, of

Stendhal, Chateaubriand, George Eliot, and the Goncourt brothers.

A collection of Proust's pastiches, *L'Affaire Lemoine*, was published in a scholarly edition, replete with extensive notes and indications of variations among the various manuscripts. It was printed in 1994 in Geneva in French by Slatkine, and edited by Jean Milly. Earlier, more readable versions exist, including the original *Pastiches et mélanges* published by Gallimard in 1919.

When Proust was just fourteen he answered the question "Your favorite occupation?" by mentioning writing verse (among other things), yet his collected poems were not published until 1982 by Gallimard in the *Cahiers Marcel Proust*.

Proust translated Ruskin's *The Bible of Amiens* in 1904 and *Sesame and Lilies* in 1906. These translations are fascinating because of Proust's voluble notes, which at some points threaten to capsize poor Ruskin. They are available in French in inexpensive and accurate paperbacks. I drew several ideas about Proust and Ruskin from the introduction by Antoine Compagnon to *Sésame et les lys*, published by Editions Complexe in 1987. Compagnon also prefaced a book composed of Proust's essays on Baudelaire, Flaubert, and Morand.

Proust's voluminous correspondence has been published (in French) by the American scholar Philip Kolb, who brought out the letters in twenty-one volumes between 1970 and 1993, published in Paris by Plon. Kolb was a tireless, brilliant scholar in the French department at the University of Illinois who dated, edited, and analyzed Proust's letters; any chronology of Proust's life owes everything to this edition of the letters, which Kolb did at the request of Proust's niece. These volumes are slowly being translated into English. There are, in addition, many separate books of Proust's letters (to Madame Straus, to his mother, to Reynaldo Hahn, to Lucien Daudet, to Gallimard, and to Jacques Rivière, just to mention a few). I particularly enjoyed a book written by Luc Fraisse in French called *Proust au miroir de sa correspondance*, published by Sedes in 1996. Fraisse organizes his book by topic ("Proust and Medicine," or "The Agnostic on the Threshold of Faith"), writes a few linking paragraphs on the subject, then cites the relevant passages from Proust's correspondence.

BIOGRAPHIES OF PROUST

The most famous biography in English (and one of the most influential biographies of the century) is George D. Painter's *Marcel Proust: A Biography*, originally published by Chatto & Windus (London) in two volumes, the first in 1959 and the second in 1964. A revised and enlarged one-volume edition came out in 1989. This book is so amusing that it could be used as a source for a stand-up comic. Indeed, Painter scoured all the memoirs of the day to extract from them the funniest bits. Oddly enough, Painter did not interview any of the many people Proust knew who were still living when he began his research. He relied entirely on the written record.

Painter seems almost obsessed with discovering who were the "originals" of Proust's characters, which can make for tiresome reading. He also has a rather mawkish and judgmental attitude towards Proust's homosexuality. We learn that Proust was "an active, not a passive invert" (rather hard to reconcile with all of Proust's affairs with straight trade such as Agostinelli and Rochat). At the end of chapter 4 Painter tells us that Proust never forgot the young girls he loved as an adolescent: ". . . When he migrated to the Cities of the Plain he took with him a prisoner crushed beneath the weight of Time and Habit, a buried heterosexual boy who continued to cry unappeased for a little girl lost." I would suggest that Proust's exclusively homosexual sexual experience might suggest that the only little girl he was crying over was inside him.

The best biography ever written of Proust is by Jean-Yves Tadié, *Marcel Proust*, published in 1996 by Gallimard and scheduled to be published in English by Penguin. When I first skimmed the 952-page text I seriously underestimated its worth, since it lacks narrative sweep and humor value and sometimes looks just like random notes (Tadié in fact did the notes for the Pléiade edition). But a careful reading reveals that this masterpiece is as thorough about the events of Proust's life as it is perceptive and comprehensive about his intellectual influences. Tadié has no preconceived psychological notions and no ambition to decode the real from the invented. What interests him most is how Proust came to write *In Search of Lost Time*, and that is the trail he traces out with myriad details. He discusses Proust's sexuality without having any Freudian biases, he deals with Proust's snobbishness without striking a morally superior tone, he reconstructs Proust's emotional and artistic evolution not from his letters (which are peculiarly impersonal) but from an intimate knowledge of what Proust was reading and of the preoccupations of the people he was meeting. Most important, Tadié has studied the manuscripts of Proust's fiction with more thoroughness and understanding than anyone else alive. I'm not at all sure that he would approve of the homosexual bias of my little book, but I'm quick to acknowledge that it owes everything to his monumental work.

Ronald Hayman's *Proust*, published in 1990, benefits from Kolb's edition of the letters and is therefore more accurate and thorough than Painter, even if the style is much more lackluster. In France, every year brings a new Proust biography; among those I consulted are *L'Impossible Marcel Proust* by Roger Duchêne, published by Laffont in 1994, and Ghislain de Diesbach's snobbish *Proust*, published by Perrin in 1991.

BOOKS ABOUT PROUST

Proust and the Art of Love: The Aesthetics of Sexuality in the Life, Times & Art of Marcel Proust, by J. E. Rivers, published by Columbia in 1980, helped me immensely in my discussions of Agostinelli and Plantevignes and Proust's sexuality in general. Lionel Povert's entry on Proust in his *Dictionnaire Gay* gave me a few invaluable details. I was taken by Walter Benjamin's remarks about Proust in his letters, published by the University of Chicago Press in 1994.

There are countless memoirs by people who knew Proust. One of the silliest is Princess Marthe Bibesco's book, *Proust's Oriane*, in which she strives to prove that the duchesse de

Guermantes is based on the comtesse de Chevigné and not on the Comtesse Greffulhe, whereas in fact the character owes something to both women and to Madame Straus as well.

I read Benoist-Méchin's padded *Avec Marcel Proust* and the painter Jacques-Emile Blanche's *Mes Modèles*, in which he has a stunning chapter on Proust. Ferdinand Bac has a ridiculous chapter on Proust in his 1935 memoir, *La Fin des "temps délicieux,"* in which he compares Proust unfavorably to the Comte Greffulhe. Bac pictures Proust as a cobra trying to charm a Gallic rooster—unsuccessfully, since Greffulhe maintains his noble impassivity and "Proust had only nibbled at the crumbs of this majestic façade. . . ."

I especially enjoyed *Trente Ans de dîners en ville* by Gabriel Louis Pringué, published in 1948, since he repeats many of the witticisms that circulated in Parisian society, often in a sharper version than the one Proust quotes, which only goes to show, as Gertrude Stein contended, that literature is not anecdotes.

Painter gives a full bibliography of memoirs about Proust. The most moving one, of course, is Céleste Albaret's *Monsieur Proust*, since it was written by his maid, who lived with him, night and day, for ten years and provides us with the most intimate portrait that we have of this generous, selfish man, this strong weakling, this compassionate snob. It was translated and published in English in 1976.

Of the hundreds of critical books available, I owe a debt to Gilles Deleuze for his *Proust and Signs*, translated in 1973. I used this semiotic text extensively in a course I taught on Proust at Columbia in 1981 at the School of the Arts. Howard Moss, an old friend and the poetry editor of *The New Yorker*, published *The Magic Lantern of Marcel Proust* in 1963, the sort of belletristic appreciation that never gets published today, alas; his was one of the first books about Proust I ever read.

All of the greatest minds from every country have been trained sooner or later on Proust. The Irish writer Samuel Beckett wrote a concise study of Proust. In Germany, Walter Benjamin. In Spain, José Ortega y Gasset, who in an essay called "Time, Distance and Form in the Art of Proust" asserts that Proust invented a new proximity between us and things, so that "nearly all literary production before him takes on an aspect of bird's-eye literature, crudely panoramic, compared to this deliciously myopic genius." In Italy, Pietro Citati. In France, everyone from Gérard Genette to Michel Leiris, from Julia Kristeva to Roland Barthes. In a short essay that was published in a special Proust issue of *Magazine Littéraire*, Barthes speculates that Proust went from being an incompetent writer of fragments to a great novelist in 1909, once he had come upon four discoveries: a peculiar way of narrating in the first person so that the "I" shifts seamlessly from the author to the Narrator to the hero; a poetic choice of evocative names for his characters after years of vacillation; a decision to "think big" and to give his book a much larger scale; and finally a novelistic sense of growth and repetition, based on what Proust called Balzac's "admirable invention of keeping the same characters in all his novels."

There are many lighter books about Proust that amused and informed me, including Alain de Botton's recent *How Proust Can Change Your Life*, a half-funny, half-serious attempt to apply Proust's moral and philosophical principles to one's own daily existence and amorous or career qualms. A big recent picture book, *Les Promenades de Marcel Proust*, enabled me to envision the places Proust was thinking of while writing, as did Henri Raczymow's *Le Paris littéraire et intime de Marcel Proust*, Ottaviani's and Poulain's *Le Paris de Marcel Proust*, and the mixture of period pictures and paragraphs from old memoirs in *Le Grand Livre de Proust*, published by Les Belles Lettres.